Beyond the Fray

A Life Story of Triumph Over Tragedy

Nicholas B. Ibarra

© 2015 Nicholas B. Ibarra

All Rights Reserved.

No part of this publication may be reproduced, stored in a retrieval system, or transmitted, in any form or by any means, electronic, mechanical, photocopying, recording, or otherwise, without the written permission of the author.

First published by Dog Ear Publishing
4011 Vincennes Rd
Indianapolis, IN 46268
www.dogearpublishing.net

ISBN: 978-1-4575-4076-9

This book is printed on acid-free paper.

Printed in the United States of America

Acknowledgments

Over the course of the past three years, I have come to know and love so many people who are now dear members of my family and my life. I would be remiss if I didn't mention them, for without them, this project wouldn't have been possible because their support was profoundly necessary for me to find a "better me."

In no order and with reference to their first names and roles only, here goes.

Beginning with family: Heavenly Father, for another chance in life; Jina, for standing beside me through the most difficult years of my life; Jina's family, for giving me a chance regardless of preconceived notions; Zack, Hailey, and Benny, for showing me what it means to have an endless capacity to love; my mom, Howard, Tia, and Cal, for being there for me—especially in the days immediately following January 1, 2012.

Next, on the business side: The employers who stood by me and/or gave me a chance when I was a liability; Jonathan R. for helping me with book edits; "the other Nick" for helping me make this happen financially; Tyson for helping me do the best I could with what I was given in court; Jared and Joanna H. for the book's head shot of me.

On the friendship side: Dave and Scott for standing up for me during discussions I wasn't present for; Mark T. for providing an inspirational example of manhood and wonderful spiritual guidance; Cheryl, Arlie, Rick, Esther, Karl, and all the others I know I'm missing who showed up to support me in court; the city council colleagues who treated my resignation with compassion; Lyle, Chris J., my cousins and aunts, and all the others who wrote me while I was incarcerated; last, but hardly least, all of the Marines I served with in Kilo Battery 3/12 and also Fox Company 2nd MPBN—brothers to the end. I'd like to give special recognition to Cindy for her ability to be there for me and to show me how to be political foes and personal friends simultaneously in the most classy way.

Lastly, I want to recognize those professionals who have helped me on my way to find a better me in life: Ray, Dan, Dwayne, Brian, Karl (again), and Darryl.

I am sure that I am missing many people, but that doesn't mean they are any less valuable to me, so thank you to the unnamed friends and family who have been in my life for better or worse.

Thanks to all,

Nick

Introduction

A quick introduction is necessary to explain the timing of the book, its events, and why the narrative may seem to change throughout.

The first nine chapters of *Beyond the Fray* were written during the better part of 2012, and Chapter 10 was written in March and April of 2014, during my incarceration for my actions discussed throughout the story. The last chapter, Chapter 11, was written during the first months of 2015. I wrote the last chapter in a different form and intent during the summer of 2014, but was later inspired to change that final chapter, allowing it to take the form it is in currently.

It is with this that I invite you to begin a story I believe is truly about the will of the human spirit and how we as a people can overcome the challenges we face through sincere faith and the help of family and true friends.

Regards,

Nick Ibarra

Song of David

The L ORD is my rock, and my fortress, and my deliverer;

The God of my rock; in him will I trust: he is my shield, and the horn of my salvation, my high tower, and my refuge, my saviour; thou savest me from violence.

I will call on the L ORD, who is worthy to be praised:
so shall I be saved from mine enemies.

When the waves of death compassed me,
the floods of ungodly men made me afraid;

The sorrows of hell compassed me about;
the snares of death prevented me;

In my distress I called upon the L ORD, and cried to my God:
and he did hear my voice out of his temple,
and my cry did enter into his ears.

2 Samuel 22

1.
Here I Am

When I became fully conscious of where I was, I felt nothing but a pit in my stomach and my mind raced with anxiety. It was New Year's Day of 2012, and the beginning of what would end up being the longest twenty-seven hours of my life.

Less than twelve hours before, I remember having so much excitement about the New Year: There was going to be the political Super Bowl of a Presidential election, with Barack Obama and Mitt Romney (who would soon become the Republican nominee) going head to head; all my friends who were state office holders were up for election; I was starting my third year as a member of city council in Springfield, Missouri; at the council level, we were going into a second round of the "smoking ban" debate, which was a highly philosophical and deeply passionate debate (something I lived for).

On the personal side I was a mess, but I did have my two kids—the two most wonderful gifts I have been given—and I had a growing relationship with the person who would end up being my best friend and, in the end, more; she showed me how to live life for the first time. That was it on the good things in life at that time.

At that time, I was dealing with a Thanksgiving Day on-the-road altercation that turned out to be very bad. (I would end up being charged with three felonies and a misdemeanor.) I felt that what was going to happen was going to happen, and there was no use in dwelling on something I couldn't undo. The incident did not cause the end of my time on city council, and that itself gave me some comfort.

In short, my life was being lived in a million different directions, but I was going to make the best of what I had been given. After all, to that point, life had been extremely intense—but that was neither here nor there; this was 2012, and I was going to make it count.

Then came the afternoon of New Year's Day. After a massively disturbing altercation with my estranged wife that ended with me having a loaded pistol in my mouth, I was put into handcuffs and taken to the county jail. After being booked, I was made to strip, put into jail clothes, and sent to an all-concrete holding room where the only things present were a toilet, sink, and "bed," which was nothing more than a concrete block that was elevated from the rest of the concrete floor.

Just a short time later, one of the guards pulled me out of my cell. He said I was going to need to change again and asked me to follow. He explained that after reviewing what happened that afternoon and some of my responses to the questions asked while being booked, they were going to have to hold me in a cell intended for suicide risks. They put me in a thick, green, one-piece vest that was similar to a full-body umpire's vest and placed me in a rubber room with absolutely nothing but a drain for me to urinate in. To do anything else, I had to be escorted to the proper facility.

Now, to keep the full picture of what was going on, I must be up front about two things—I was appreciative, for one, and it did allow me to take away a story that makes most others laugh…and at this point, it makes me laugh as well.

I was appreciative of the rubber room. The blanket, which was made from the same material as my vest, was much warmer than the T-shirt thin sheets in the concrete room; the rubber bed and room itself was much warmer than the concrete-bed cell, as well. I was able to doze off for bits at a time in relative comfort, given the circumstances.

I couldn't laugh then, but now I'm appreciative of the laugh I get in looking back at breakfast. The night before, I was given dinner but was so emotionally high-strung and dealing with a hangover that for me, eating was not an option. When breakfast came I was more than ready. They served me with a Styrofoam container similar to a to-go box in a restaurant. On top of it was a single serving of milk in a cardboard container similar to what one would find in a cafeteria in grade school. The first thought I had was that the water I had been given was no longer appealing and milk sounded like a perfect alternative. I drank it immediately and remember how good it felt going down. Then I opened my container to find some fruit and...cereal. Seriously?! Of all things that could happen, could it get any worse than me drinking the milk for my cereal because I didn't know about the cereal?! *Unbelievable*, I thought as I ate my fruit and dry cereal. You can thank me for the entertaining story, and it's funny in hindsight, but on January 2, 2012, there was nothing funny about it.

So, there I was, sitting in a jail cell, hung over, scared of the future, realizing the gravity of the situation, and ashamed of the man I had become. I had let myself, my community, and my children down, and I was sure the Lord was not pleased with me, either.

I thought of who I was on the inside versus who I was on the outside; I realized that the person I believed I was wasn't the person the outside world was seeing all over the local news. Then I thought, *What if I'm not who I think I am or want to be, but rather a person that actually belongs here in jail?* That couldn't be, though. I had a good heart; I meant well; I wanted to help others and couldn't fathom doing any harm to an innocent individual. While that was the case, the decisions I had made in the past forty-five days had landed me in a rubber room with only a drain for a toilet.

Pondering further, I decided that this was not who I was; it was in that jail cell and over the next twenty-seven hours that I decided the situation had to change. I was a former US Marine and Iraq veteran who'd completed forty-seven convoy missions, a father, a community servant, and a man who graduated with a 3.913 cumulative GPA from a private university; I was an elected official in the third largest city in Missouri, and most of all I loved the Lord and believed He gave His only son so that I may be forgiven. I had definitely strayed, but I loved the Lord and was ashamed because I knew He was not pleased with me.

That is when it came to me: "Here I am. All that I am, all that I've done, all that I have achieved—I am now nothing more than a man in a suicide-risk jail cell with no idea what the future holds for me." Quite a gravitating thought to have in your heart and mind for what seems like an eternity.

When I got out of jail on the evening of the second, I realized a few things that have stuck with me, but one of the most important things is this: I am a man who is full of faults, but my life was not over and I wasn't out of chances—it was going to be what I made it.

I was soon told I was a veteran who needed to ask for help because of both my experience in Iraq and several things I experienced as a child. I was told I couldn't take another drink of alcohol for the rest of my life because of the adverse affects it had on my decision-making skills. I needed to work on restoring my standing with myself, my family and friends, society, and the Lord, and once that trust was back, I was to never take it for granted again.

As we will discuss, music has had a profound impact on my life, so we'll conclude this chapter with a musical reference. There is a heavy metal band that goes by the name of Hatebreed. Ironically, much of their message is about overcoming obstacles and adversity and never letting life get the best of you. In one particular song, "You're Never Alone," there is a phrase that so well describes where I was and, to be successful in restoring what I had lost, I would have to live by: "It's our struggles that define us."

Was I going to learn from this experience, or was I going to let it get the best of me? Was I going to grow from and overcome this experience or let it become an excuse for later failures? Was I going to make the best of the position I was in and allow it to make me a better person, or was I going to say, "I'm done trying to achieve success in life?" When I asked myself those three questions that day, my answer was the former option all three times.

It was with the knowledge that life would never be the same and that my immediate future held nothing but difficult situations and decisions that I emerged from jail on the night of January 2, 2012. It was also with the determination that I would grow from the experience and that I would overcome the obstacles. I also determined that throughout the process I would learn about a different way of life as I took those steps away from county corrections into a life that would never be the same.

2.
A Short Biography

I was born December 9, 1979 in Chula Vista, California, a suburb of San Diego. My father (Lawrence) was a career Navy enlisted man, and my mother (Cheryl), after being in the Navy for several years, spent most of her career working for the federal government in finance.

For the first several years of my life, I lived in California, New Mexico, and Virginia. In 1983, while living in New Mexico on White Sands Missile Range, my brother was born. I still remember the first time I saw him—he was in the hospital's plastic "crib" set beside my mother's hospital bed. The name decided was Zachary Charles. On the way home from the hospital after he was born, he got sick and I asked if we were going to have to take him back since he was "broken." Thankfully, my parents didn't see that as an option!

In 1985 my father retired from the Navy and began work with Hughes Aircraft Company. While the position was initially in Las Cruces, about a half-hour away from White Sands Missile Range, he was soon transferred to Long Beach, California.

Until 1989, life was what you would expect for a typical American family.

In 1989, my father was required to get a physical for work purposes. This was the beginning of several events that led to him being diagnosed with acute promyelocytic leukemia. For several years he was in and out of the hospital for chemotherapy, and finally, in January of 1993, he lost his battle with cancer. He now rests at Ft. Sam Houston in Texas with his father and other family members who served this great nation.

Within a couple of months my mother moved us to Springfield, Missouri. She said she wanted to be close to her family and where she grew up in Independence, Missouri, but far enough away that they had to call before coming over...reasonable logic, if you ask me. My now-stepfather (Howard) came with us and has been my mother's partner ever since.

After moving in the late spring, the unimaginable happened. In June, my brother, ten years old at the time, was killed in a traffic accident. After that, and understandably so, my mother "checked out" of sane and rational living. I lived with my aunt for approximately one year (for the eighth grade and the beginning of my freshman year) in St. Louis due to the inability of my mother to take care of me. After the first few months of my freshman year in high school, I returned home to my mother in Springfield.

In high school I didn't have a problem making friends, but at the same time I was never the "social" type. The Christmas of my freshman year I was given my first set of drums, and my steadfast goal was to learn as much as possible as soon as possible. Howard, my stepfather, was a local musician who was playing seven nights a week at the time, and I wanted to be on the stage with him. After several months of nothing but drumming outside of school and homework, I was given the opportunity to play with him; I ended up playing music with him for the remainder of my high school years.

In February of 1997 I met Kara. It was my junior and her sophomore year of high school, and we dated for the rest of the school year and into the beginning of the summer. That summer she became pregnant with my son Zachary Thomas. (Zachary was my brother's name and Thomas was the name of a cousin who also passed away in an automobile accident during my high-school years.) He was born

March 3, 1998. He has been such a blessing, and I love him so much—words can't explain how thankful I am to my Heavenly Father for what he gave me in my son.

The summer after graduation I left for Marine boot camp. After boot camp and my military occupational schooling, Kara and I married. We spent the next four years stationed at Camp Pendleton in Southern California.

The main memory I have of Camp Pendleton was the time spent with friends I'll never forget. When I was a child, my mother would tell me stories of how she and my father would invite all the single sailors over for barbeques and quality time outside the barracks—a proxy adoption of sorts for young sailors who were far from home. I carried that tradition with me. Scott, Brad, Greg, Chad, Jimmy, Eddie... every weekend we would go to the beach and then make our way back to base housing for barbeque, football games, and movies.

While on active duty I was attached to Kilo Battery, 3 Battalion/12 Marine Regiment—an artillery unit. While the Marine Corps was a memory in and of itself, being in artillery was what made it all the more unique. So much time was spent away from family, whether in the field or out of country, that those fellows next to me became my family, my brothers.

After ten years of touch-and-go contact, I recently attended Scott's wedding. Brad was there, and it was a wonderful experience…Though ten years had passed, it seemed as if we hadn't lost a second. It was wonderful. I also keep in touch with Chad regularly, and when he makes his way home to Kansas City from Pennsylvania, we try and get together for at least an evening. The rest of my brothers are so close to my heart that if they called at 2:00 AM and needed something, if at all possible, I would be there; I believe they would do the same for me. The Marine Corps is an eternal brotherhood, and the experience was one I wouldn't trade for anything.

During my stay in California, I met the most beautiful girl in the world. She was born on July 7, 2000, and her name is Hailey Breann. She is such a wonderful little girl—though she is becoming "not so little" as I type these words—but no matter how old she is or what she does, there is no more beautiful sound in the world than her saying the word "Daddy."

After I was honorably discharged in 2002, I stayed in California. I had taken up playing music with Brad and Chad and we had come across Rob, a young guitarist who could do things with the six-string that I had never seen done in person. Because of the financial hardship that getting out of the service created and growing marital difficulties, Kara and the kids moved back to Missouri and Kara and I separated. I stayed in Southern California and worked for a fabrication and distribution company and continued to play music.

The band I played with ended up winning an award for Best San Diego Band and was nominated for another regional award; we were also lucky enough to play some really unique shows, including Whiskey A Go Go on the Sunset Strip—a stage on which the Rolling Stones, Janis Joplin, Metallica, and many other big names started their careers.

In the summer of 2003, when it was clear that Kara was staying in Missouri, I left California and moved back to Missouri to be with the kids. Chad, Brad, and Rob moved to Pennsylvania to continue their efforts in the music industry.

Back in Springfield, Kara and I began to try and work things out. The difficult part was that we had both considered ourselves separated, so it was more of a case of "getting back together" than it was working things out. I took employment at St. John's (now Mercy) Hospital and started going to community college.

When I got out of the Marines, our military had been in Afghanistan for several months; immediately following my discharge, they were heading to Iraq, so it goes without saying that many of my friends who were still in the service went overseas. As I continued to go to college and work, I began to feel the need to go back into the service. I felt, quite frankly, like a football player who left the team the season before the Super Bowl, and regret weighed heavily on my heart. As time passed, the weight of that regret grew heavier with each news report I watched, so being *Semper Fi*, I called a prior-service recruiter. "I want to re-enlist, and I want to do so with a unit that is headed to Iraq. I don't want to be with some unit that is going to sit on a base and turn wrenches, either. I want to see what this is about, and I mean it."

I got my wish. I still remember a moment a few days before I left when I was riding in the car with Zack and Hailey and listening to "American Soldier," a country song by Toby Keith. While Hailey was there, she was only four years old and didn't completely understand what was going on. Zack, though, was as fully aware of the gravity of the situation as a six year old could be. We cried and held hands as we listened to the song. A couple days later we were at the airport and saying our goodbyes. As I left and went through the security check after I said my goodbyes, I looked back. My then father-in-law was holding Zack back as he was crying and trying to fight him and get to me one more time. While the plane was taxiing on the runway, I was only able to partially take in the fact that "this was it." Regardless of how much I could or couldn't grasp it, the fact remained that taking to the sky that day began a journey that forever changed who I was, what I believed, and how I viewed life.

I was attached to 1st Platoon, Fox Company, 2nd Military Police Battalion, whose primary responsibility was convoy security. I remember the day we got on the plane from South Carolina to make our way to Kuwait and eventually Iraq. We had taken off from the ground, and I realized that that moment may have been the last time I would see the United States of America. As we took off, Corporal Davis Cavalier, who ended up being a really good friend, looked at me and said, "It's just us now; we have nobody but each other." This was his second tour, and I was soon to recognize the wisdom of his words.

We arrived in Iraq in March of 2005. I remember taking the helicopter from the air base to the camp we were going to be based. We flew directly over Fallujah, at that time one of the hottest spots in country, only several months after the second major battle in the city had taken place. It was a sobering experience. I remember thinking, *Alright, you asked for what you wanted and you got it...There is no reset, and there aren't three lives before the game is over. Do your job, and do it as good as you possibly can.*

During my time in Iraq, I was able to participate in forty-seven missions—our platoon was tasked primarily with covering convoys that required some sort of security on the open road. I remember a particular mission here and a mission there, but outside of the "memorable" missions, they all seemed to run together after a while. We mainly did equipment transportation security, but we also did troop transportation and prisoner transportation and/or release. We operated out of al-Anbar Province; we did many of our missions in Fallujah, Ramadi, to and from Baghdad International Airport, and to the Syrian and Jordanian borders. Over the course of our missions, we were hit (the term used when enemy contact is made directly or indirectly—roadside bombs, for instance) many times—I think I stopped counting at ten. It is interesting what the human mind can come to rationalize as normal. I will touch on this in a later chapter in more detail. The experience I had overseas was one that I wouldn't change for anything, but I would not choose to experience it again for $1,000,000.

We made our way home in October of 2005. I remember two things about the trip home: Getting on the first plane and getting off the last. There, on the runway of al-Taquaddam Airbase, I remember feeling so blessed to be one of the men who came and saw and was able to go home. My heart ached for those who never made the trip home; for their families and friends; and for their children, who would only know the stories of their personal heroes—those fathers, mothers, sons, daughters, uncles, aunts, brothers, sisters...the men and women who took their last breath in a country far from home.

I also remember getting off the last plane in Springfield—finally getting home. I stepped off the plane and into the terminal. I remember being frightened at the fact that I was about to see my family after so much had happened. I was uncomfortable with the idea that they may see me as a different person, that I would not be able to show the affection I desired to show, that I would be distant.

That all seemed to change the second I approached the bottom of the escalators that led to the baggage claim area. There I was in my desert fatigues, walking as fast as I could to the crowd gathered with signs and cameras. The first person I saw was my son, then my daughter—they ran up and gave me a hug, and we cried together. It was a hug I'll never forget; they were the two best hugs I have ever received and probably ever will. I have a picture of that hug framed and on my desk at work to this day.

It wasn't long before I was discharged from the Marines for the second time. I took up work in a warehouse that fabricated industrial products. After less than a year I was promoted to sales representative and stayed in that position until I left the company in the fall of 2010.

During my time with that particular company, I became involved in local politics and made the decision to run for city council in Springfield, Missouri. I ran as a vocal opponent of many city council policies at a time when community discontent with municipal government was prevalent. For one year and five months, I spent a majority of my time knocking on the doors of constituents and fundraising for campaign advertisement. In April of 2009 I was elected to represent one-quarter of the city—the northwest area of Springfield, Missouri.

Over the next two years and eight months, there were several issues that came to the forefront at the local level. The new council—all members were either newly in office or had only been in office two years—faced a pension fund problem for the police and fire departments' retirement. After years of bad judgment and negligence, the funds were almost $200 million in the red. The annual city budget at the time was barely larger than that. The general trust with the community was at a very low level. The previous council was known to be pretentious on several occasions and led the city in a ruling-class elitist manner.

With the new council, the most important thing we cared about was transparency. We may not have always made the best decisions, but the decisions we made were in public, and we were always willing to answer to the constituents—a drastic change from the previous council, and one that had very positive results. I still remember how good it felt every time I would do something, no matter how small, and be thanked for it. There were instances where I had curb and gutter renovations done or streetlights installed and the constituents would tell me how they had been trying to get those things done for years and nobody would help. Even though many of the acts that I promoted took little effort on my part, I felt that I was being successful in my service to the community.

There were bigger issues, as well. Whether it was a zoning issue that had an entire neighborhood irate about how it would affect their properties or a smoking ban that would bring out philosophical passion in which property rights and public health were pitted against each other, there was no shortage of issues facing the community. As a council we were always transparent about how we felt, and our Mayor, Mayor Jim O'Neal, was a driving force in letting the voices of the council be heard. Let it be said that as mayor, he always had the last word, and it was often directed at me (we didn't see things eye to eye on several occasions…okay, most occasions), but the fact of matter is that he never once tried to stifle my thoughts or those of any others on the council. That, along with the amount of attention we all paid to the needs and desires of the community as a whole, brought a sense of transparency that was long overdue in a community that had been subject to previous municipal leaders who carried on in a manner not very accommodating to those they were supposed to represent.

During my tenure on the council, my marriage began to unravel more than it already had prior to my election. Kara and I had been married for several years, and most of those years were spent fighting or apart (military deployments for the most part, save one year with me in California and her in Missouri). In the spring of 2011 we separated for the final time. I firmly believe that we are two people who differ on every level, from what to cook for dinner to how to raise Zack and Hailey. When I left that spring, I believed (and still do) that there were no other options at that point.

Several months passed, and the adjustment of the separation took place. I was staying with my mother and stepfather while getting on my feet and working at the place of employment I had started the October before, and I continued to work diligently on the council.

Then came the holiday season of 2011; this was a forty day window that would forever change my life. The first incident happened on Thanksgiving afternoon. I was at my mother's for an early dinner and was to leave for time with the kids. I was on my way from the east side to the west side of town when I came in contact with an individual driving erratically. The drive-turned-confrontation will be discussed later in more detail, but a short explanation here is in order: The media reported what happened as a "road rage incident" that involved "a city councilman." I was driving through town and came into confrontation with another driver on the road. It ended up with me following him home. While there, a confrontation ensued that involved what the media described as me dragging two people in/on my vehicle down the road while I left the area. I was unable to make any sort of statement with regard to the incident per my legal counsel's advice, so the media could do and say what they needed in order to do their job without me being able to discuss my side of the story whatsoever. After the investigation I was charged with three counts of felony assault and one count of tampering with evidence.

The next occurrence took place on New Year's Day of 2012. By nightfall, I was in a jail cell waiting to be charged with one more felony count. It involved a confrontation that happened between Kara and me. I will later discuss the events that happened, and I will also discuss the psychology of what I was going through during that time in great detail. After that experience, I had another felony added to my charges: Unlawful use of a weapon.

Again, there will be detailed discussion of these two events later in the book, but I would be remiss if I didn't mention them in this short introductory biography for the reason of their profound impact on my life since.

After getting out of the county jail, I knew that things had to change. I still remember sitting down to write my resignation letter to Mayor O'Neal. I thought to myself that there had been two times in my adult life when I had quit. The first was my marriage, and the second was to now be my position on city council.

After the resignation, I had the time to begin self-reflection and the sorting out of life on the terms my new life presented. The most interesting part is that I felt hopeful. I knew the road ahead was not going to be an easy one, but I was okay as long as my Heavenly Father and his Son could look on me with approval and as long as my children were in my life and I could be a better father than I had in the past. Lastly, I needed and received help from my best friend, who accepted me at my weakest point and wasn't afraid to be there for me. It's with those things that I believed there was nothing unmanageable, nothing unattainable, and nothing that could stop the progress of me becoming a better man.

3.
To Prove What?

I still remember it as clear as day: I was sitting in my room my senior year of high school and arguing with my mother. I don't recall the substance of the argument, but I do remember her comment, which is engraved in my memory: "If you even make it in the Marines, you won't make a good one."

I had joined the US Marines Delayed Entry Program several months before. Delayed entry is a program the military offers to young people who desire to join the military but have to complete something—high school, for instance. The program is intended to prepare the future service member for boot camp and give them a better understanding of the military life of which they will be a part.

I had been in the program since the beginning of the summer before my senior year in high school. The Marines were the branch I had pretty much settled on before walking into any recruiter's office, but the Marine recruiter himself was quite the salesman. Sergeant O'Donnell was his name, and his sales pitch was quite persuasive: "Look, Nick, it's simple. You can be *in* the Army, you can be *in* the Air Force, you can be *in* the Navy, or you can *be* a Marine."

Sold to the idealist kid who wanted to make a difference in the world!

The words that my mother stated soon after I entered the delayed entry program, though they were spoken in anger and hostility, were devastating as they reverberated in my mind—"If you even make it in the Marines, you won't make a good one."

This wasn't the first time somebody told me of the failure I was sure to become.

I remember my second grade teacher; she was a real charmer. So much so that she told my mother and father that I would end up in prison. What a great amount of faith she had in me. That's right, there are were second grade teachers in this world who tell parents which children will end up in prison.

Thank God for my third grade teacher, Mrs. Alexander. She was the teacher who allowed you to dream and then reinforced those dreams by encouraging you to follow them with determination. I went from being a future convict to the future President of the United States in one year—Mrs. Alexander was sure of it.

The point I'm making is that we all go through life, sometimes beginning young, while having people make judgments about us. Sometimes they are good, and sometimes they are bad. For many years, all I concentrated on was the bad: My teacher said I would be a convict; my aunt told me I would never graduate high school or amount to anything; a high school coach indirectly told me I wouldn't make it in the Marines. At no other time in life have I been more devastated than when my mother, in my room and in that argument, told me that *if* I made it to the Marines I wouldn't make a good one.

Don't get me wrong; I love my mother with all my heart, and we have had a life full of struggles. I can't think of another life warrior I would want to go through that with if I had to go through it the way that I have, but the point of reviewing this part of my past is this: For all the years I was given negativity from judgmental individuals around me, I doubled my efforts and spent twice that amount of time trying to prove them wrong…Or was I trying to prove myself right, to prove my value and my abilities? Regardless of the answer, I worked as hard as possible to make sure everything I did was done with my best efforts given.

Looking back, I believe I did the best I could with the tools I was given.

My son was born three months before I graduated high school; but I was not going to let that stop me from graduating. I saw many of my peers having children while still in school and using that as a crutch – an excuse – to allow failure to creep in. I was not going to be the person who did that.

In the Marines I was no "stellar performer." I didn't win any awards or get any special recognition until the last year of my initial active-duty tour. It wasn't that I didn't want to, rather that I was never put in the situation of having to until a man I still consider one of the best friends I have ever had, Scott (then Corporal) White, left the artillery unit to which I was attached during my initial active-duty service. He was my section leader as well as my friend, and he taught me what being a good Marine was about.

When he left, I was the next in command of our section. At the rank of corporal, I was to fulfill the billet (position) of a staff sergeant—a rank two above mine. I only filled it for about six months, but during that time, major training exercises took place and I was responsible for men, vehicles, artillery ammunition, and tactical movements. For my performance I was awarded the Navy and Marine Achievement Medal (NAM); the NAM is one of the more distinguished medals one can receive when not in a combat situation. I say this not to boast or brag; I did what I was supposed to, and there are many men who have done much greater things. To me, it was proof that all those who said I would make anything less than a good Marine had been proved wrong.

About a year before my active duty stint ended, I joined a heavy metal band. All four members were in the same military unit. Soon it became apparent that our guitarist was not on the same page as Chad (vocals), Brad (bass), and I (drums) with regard to what we wanted to do as a band both in style and in how far we were willing to take the project. He was more interested in the influences of Nirvana and the grunge era, whereas the rest of us were seeking a more metal sound like that of Pantera and Slayer. He was interested in playing locally and as more of a hobby, where the three of us were willing to "go platinum" if the opportunity presented itself. In short order, we cordially separated from our guitarist and were left to find one that was more our style.

We found him, and he was a teenage kid who was just out of high school, but could do things with a guitar that are were beyond rare, all to our surprise, given that he just walked in off the street. Rob—or "Bobby," as we called him—completed the band, and we were ready to get moving. Soon we had a CD recorded and were playing venues everywhere from South San Diego to Los Angeles.

In time we were given two experiences that made me realize, once again, that when I set out to do things, I set out to rise above mediocrity and gain maximum achievement. In 2003 we were given the award for Best San Diego Band by a Southern California music magazine. Not too long after that we were given the opportunity to play at the Whiskey a Go Go on the Sunset Strip. This was the climax of our career—we played in the venue that once showcased the Doors, Jimi Hendrix, and Metallica, along with countless other music legends.

It wasn't long after that I left California to return to Springfield, Missouri to be with my children.

After arriving home I started going to college at Ozarks Technical Community College. Once again I found myself looking to prove wrong those who said I would never make anything of myself. After two years of community college I transferred to Evangel University, where I completed my bachelor's degree in business management. During my four years in school (though I was on the seven-year plan), my goal rose above just graduating. Once I realized I was good at the "college thing," I thought I would shoot for a 4.0 cumulative GPA. I fell short by making two Bs and ending with a 3.913 instead, but the point is that while I would strive to get one A after another, it wasn't for any other reason than to prove to those who forever called me less than intelligent that they were wrong!

Over the course of time, I have found that—for me, anyhow—this was the wrong approach to these things, these achievements I'd made. I didn't have the ability to live for the means because I was too consumed with the ends, with being able to put another notch on my belt of proof that I was right and everybody who disagreed with me was wrong.

Through reflection I have found that it is only to God and to myself that I am responsible to prove my worth. I want to be the best husband possible. I want to be a great father—the best father I can possibly be. I want to be a virtuous Christian, to set an example so righteous that people are forced to ask, "Something is different about you—what is it?" I want to be many things, but I have come to realize that I have to find within myself how to do that for me and for those around me whom I love and not for the ability to prove somebody else wrong.

Over the course of time and through life's experiences, I have come to realize that I was looking through the prism of life in a way that I don't care to any longer; I want to be able to live in the moment and cherish the gifts that have been given to me by God—my family, my health, my work, my friends, and my surroundings. To do this—for myself and in each of life's moments—is to find an acceptance of being who I am and being satisfied with the person I have now become. I now feel free to enjoy life without letting my past experiences dampen my outlook and daily approach to life, and I can make the best of what I hope to look back on as the "good ole days." Somebody once said to me that life is about the journey and not the destination—good advice that I have learned to try to abide by daily.

4.
Defining Moments

Not very long ago I watched *The Vow*. It is a movie about a married couple who was in an automobile accident; the wife was without a seatbelt when it happened. She survived but suffered from severe memory loss—she didn't remember her husband or much of her adult life. The movie is about the husband trying his hardest to help her readjust and move forward in life. In the movie, he calls profound events in life such as this "moments of impact." These are the events that happen, many times quickly and unexpectedly, that completely change your outlook on life and what it means. While the example in the movie may be negative, there can be positive ones, as well, such as children being born and marriages (but to a large degree, those things are expected).

While the husband in the movie calls them "moments of impact," I have always called the same type of situation a "defining moment"—that moment in life when you realize you will never be the same. I have had several defining moments that shaped who I am and how I perceive life. At the same time these moments have made me stronger (a favorite saying among Marines is that if it doesn't kill you, it only makes you stronger), they have also been a curse—not only have many of the events been traumatic, but they have also often made me callous to the hardships of others, primarily when the hardships were used as a crutch. However, when I came across those actually in the fray of a hardship, I have always been of service and helpful when given the opportunity. I am also not afraid to share how I feel about the fact that our struggles define us and that the future is still in our control much of the time. That is the most important factor in the way I view defining moments: What we do after—how we recover, how we face the fight—is what defines man's character.

Given this book's intent, I thought it pertinent to share some of my defining moments in hopes that even one reader may take away the fact that bad things can happen to good people but that the ability to remain good, to overcome, and to deal with life's obstacles is possible. It is simply about discipline, determination, will, and the desire to succeed; failure can't be an option, and neither can losing faith in God or what he can do in our lives.

* *

It was right around 5:00 AM on January 25, 1993, just over a month after my thirteenth birthday. I remember my mother waking me up and saying, "Nick, let's wake up; it's time to go."

"Is it over?" I questioned in response.

"Yes, honey, it's over. It's time to go."

I got up from the two waiting room chairs that were pushed together into a makeshift bed and got into the elevator with my mother, brother, and Aunt Veronica—Tia Roni, as she is endearingly known. When we left UCLA Medical Center that morning, we left the life that I had known to that point. After a four-year fight with leukemia, my father, my hero, a veteran of the US Navy and the Vietnam War, a man who wore a suit to work but didn't mind being silly at the dinner table, a man who taught me about so many things in such a little time, was gone from my life.

I remember the last conversation I had with my father. I was getting ready to leave the house and make my way to school, so I was in a hurry and not very accommodating of the directions my mother and father were giving me about daily life. I do remember, however, that my father was bed-ridden and that I leaned over to hug and kiss him.

He said, "Nick, do good in school today." I gave him positive acknowledgment and left. That afternoon my mother called and said that his regular appointment at the hospital had turned into a several-day stay so testing could be done because he had fallen in the bathroom at the hospital on his way to check-in. I talked to him briefly on the phone, but I don't remember the conversation. A few days later, my aunt flew in from Texas. She and my mother broke the news to my brother and me that Dad wasn't going to make it through the night; after the news was given, we headed to the hospital for the evening.

I chose not to see him in the hospital because, as I put it to my mother, I wanted to remember the father he was and not the man leaving this earth in a hospital bed. I still grapple with whether that was the right decision, but often lean to the thought that it was. Rather than remembering him in a hospital bed and hardwired for the final call, I remember him running sprints with me on the beach; I remember the ski trip I took with him and my brother; I remember running past all my teammates to hug him when I hit my first in-field home run; I remember the trip to the Grand Canyon; I remember him coaching every sports team I played on until he could no longer do it.

That was over that early morning, and the time to realize the need for mandatory adjustment had approached. I will always remember and forever honor the man that Lawrence Joe Ibarra was, but unfortunately, the mourning was not long-lived before another defining moment took life by the grips.

* *

Soon after my father passed away, my mother made the decision to relocate to Springfield, Missouri. As stated before, she was originally from the Kansas City area and still had family there as well as in St. Louis.

We made the move with Howard, the man who would eventually become my stepfather, and did so in a piecemeal way. The first piece was to get my brother Zack and me to Springfield. We made the trip by plane and waited for my mother and Howard to pack up the house and make the drive from Long Beach, California. We arrived in Springfield in the middle of May and stayed with Hazael, who had been my mother's best friend since elementary school. Her son Jeff was a year younger than me, making him two years older than Zack. With him there, we quickly became acclimated to the teen society that Springfield offered.

We'd been there a couple of weeks when my mother and Howard arrived. We made the move into the new house on S. Pickwick, right by Missouri State University and the downtown area. It wasn't long before we made a trip to St. Louis to visit my mother's siblings and their families; among them, Zack and I had a total of five cousins. Of them, Danny was the only male that we were around on regular basis who was close to my and my brother's age. He was of average height and red headed, but had a rather masculine stature for only being thirteen—he "worked out." The other cousins were female, older, or didn't come around much. After a several-day visit, Danny ended up coming back to Springfield with my part of the family to visit with us for part of the summer.

It wasn't long before we came upon June 30, 1993. I remember my mother and stepfather waking me up early that morning to tell me they were leaving to take care of some errands for the day. Danny was still visiting, and Hazael's son Jeff had stayed the night. Four boys were lined up on the floor in a camping-style setting, Zack at the end furthest from her. My mother said, "I'm not going to walk over everybody to tell Zack bye, but tell him I love him when he wakes up." I don't remember if I ever did. After she told me she was leaving, I fell asleep again.

When we finally woke for the day, I remember having water gun fights around the house for a short while after breakfast. The humidity of June in Missouri makes water gun fights, even in the morning, a refreshing activity. After that, we decided to go to the music store. There was a new cassette tape I wanted and figured there was no time like the present to buy it. We searched the *Yellow Pages* and called around for the first store that had it. When we found that store, we made our way there on our bikes, not realizing the store was clear across town. We got on the road, ready to ride, and quickly realized the commitment we had made.

We made our way across town on the busier streets of the city. Finally, while on Battlefield Road headed west, I saw in the distance the music store we were searching for. We were on the wrong side of the street to get to the store. Three of us crossed the street on our bikes and started down the road, but Battlefield is one of the busier roads of the city, and because of this, Zack hopped off his bike to walk it across the street—he was a steward of safe practices. I turned around to see why he was taking so long and yelled, "Quit being a wimp and let's go!"

He crossed the street, and we began the final stretch to the music store. As we got to the intersection of Battlefield and Jefferson, the light was red for east/west traffic (the traffic on Battlefield). Because there was no traffic on Jefferson, which had the green light, I decided to make my way across. Because I was on the street, I hugged the curb to squeeze between the curb itself and a semitruck that was waiting at the red light to get to the street crossing. As I squeezed through, I remember thinking, *Wow, that was kind of risky.*

Right about that time, I heard what sounded like a moan. I had mostly made my way across Jefferson, but I stopped and turned around. What I saw put me in immediate shock. The light had turned green for Battlefield at the same time Zack was trying to make his way between the curb and the truck just as I had. Nobody is sure what happened, but the investigation reports stated that Zack was spooked and fell over, ending up in the path of the truck's wheels. My first sight of the situation was the truck on top of him as he lay face down, his legs sticking out from the side of the truck.

I immediately jumped off my bike and started waving my hands for the truck to stop; the driver did so. Unfortunately, he stopped while still on top of Zack. I waved at him to move forward, and he did this until he was over and off of Zack's body. The next thing I saw was Zack getting up on his hands and knees.

As a thirteen year old who just watched his ten-year-old brother get run over and then saw him on his hands and knees, my mind—in shock—said, *Alright, he's okay. He can just get up, and we can go home. We don't even have to tell Mom what happened.* As those thoughts were passing, Zack looked up toward the sky while still on his hands and knees and then rolled over and collapsed.

Danny ran over to him and tried to pick him up as I finished making my way to the two of them. Zack was cut open from the bottom of his chest cavity to his groin area, and in the several seconds that had taken place, he was already very blue. I ran across the street to the Blockbuster Video movie store and told the clerk to call 911 because my brother had just been hit by a truck. I remember that the clerk looked at me like I was stupid. Out of nowhere, an adult—a heavyset man—was beside me and said to the clerk, "You need to call 911. He is not playing around."

After that, the people who had stopped because of the accident were not letting me see my brother. They told me I didn't need to see what was going on. The next thing I remember is being in the passenger seat of a stationary emergency vehicle. I asked a firefighter if Zack was going to be okay. I remember his words: "Buddy, I don't know. He's cut pretty bad."

Soon I found myself on the phone with my mother. I remember telling her she needed to meet me at the local hospital, St. John's Hospital, because that was where they were taking Zack. I explained that Zack had been hit by a truck and they were taking him to the hospital by ambulance. "My Zack?" she asked in screaming desperation. Soon, Howard was at the scene to pick up Danny, Jeff, and me. We met my mother in a waiting room in the hospital. I remember sitting there in shock; Danny, Jeff, and I just sat there without saying a word. A morbid sense of silence filled the room.

Jeff's stepfather Mike met us there—he was a psychologist at the hospital. While he was talking to my mother about what was going on in the operating room, I left to use the restroom. I didn't even need to use the restroom; I just needed to leave the room. After a minute in the stall, Mike came in.

"Nick, are you in here?"

"Yes."

"Let's go; we need to get back to the waiting room."

"Is everything going to be okay?"

"We just need to get back to the waiting room."

As I entered the waiting room, I felt and witnessed the horrible scene of a mother in shock and grief after finding out her youngest son would never look her in the eyes again. He was gone.

I remember entering the ER operating room that afternoon. It was cold both in temperature and in spirit. I remember crying and rubbing Zack's lifeless head. "It should have been me," I whispered. The last clear memory I have of being in the hospital that afternoon is seeing a young nurse in the room with us sobbing uncontrollably.

Looking back, it is hard to recall particular times in life I had with my brother. While I remember the abstract memories, I don't remember the small details. While I decided not to see my father in the end so I could remember the hero he was to me, I didn't have that option with Zack.

Six months and five days after losing my father, I was once again walking out of a hospital with one less member of my family. Again, I knew that life would never be the same for me.

* *

While I believe the obvious should sometimes go unstated, it is nothing but an honor to say that being a father is without doubt a life-shaping event. When considering the scripture, we are told that man must come unto the Father as a mortal child comes unto his mortal father. Consider this: How hard is it to actually receive our Heavenly Father as a child receives a parent on Earth? To have full reliance, faith, and trust in one human being; to have nothing but innocence in all that is done; to completely surrender yourself and all you are to another—that's pretty spectacular. That's why it is astonishing for me to know that I have had that experience two times—the first in 1998 and the second in 2000. As our children grow, we begin to see personalities, characteristics, and likes and dislikes. We get to see the human growth experience before our eyes and know that we play a direct role in it. I say "we" to encompass all who read and know what it is like to be called mom or dad. To know that I have been a person who has been given the full trust, reliance, and confidence of another is without doubt a phenomenal, beautiful, and defining moment and continues to be each and every day.

**

In October of 1998, I remember standing on top of the Reaper. The Reaper was a small mountain in Southern California that was the end of the rite of passage for young men who desired to carry the title of United States Marine.

After three months of drill (marching), running, drill, eating, drill, taking classes, shooting rifles, field training, and more drill, I was on top of the Reaper, tired from fifty-plus hours of little sleep and lots of rigorous combat simulation, and ready to claim the title. I was very emotional. I will never forget Drill Instructor Staff Sergeant Hawes, who was one mean drill instructor, handing me the Marine emblem—an eagle, globe, and anchor—in the form of a pendant and telling me to stop getting all teary eyed because we still had to hump (hiking with about fifty to seventy pounds of gear on your body) back to the barracks. The best part of his order was that it was preceded by him calling me "Marine." His directive to "man up" was of no consequence to my emotions at that time; I had become a Marine—a title that would remain for the rest of my life—something that could not be taken away. I was part of a brotherhood that lands first in the combat zone, a group of individuals whose history reads of battle victories with eight-to-one odds stacked against them, and a group of individuals whose motto is "honor, courage, commitment" and in which integrity—being true to self and others even when those others aren't watching—is a key principle of life.

**

The next two defining moments I will discuss are situations I experienced in Iraq. As a veteran of that war and somebody who will consider himself a sergeant in the Marine Corps until the last breath I take in my mortal existence, the years I spent in the Marines are ones that will forever be a part of me, and I truly believe I will miss them for the rest of my life.

**

It was May 10, 2005, and I was a corporal. It was our third month in the operating field of Iraq, and our mission as a company was convoy security in al-Anbar Province. The province encompasses Fallujah (where our company was based), Ramadi, Haditha and stretches as far west as the Syrian and Jordanian borders. Baghdad is just east of the province.

We had been participating in missions for about two months by May, so we were beginning to get used to being on the road and in what we called "Indian Territory." Once we were outside of the compound that was semi-secured, we were on our own. We had ten vehicles, about forty Marines, one Navy corpsman (medic), communications to call in air support if needed, and a lot of small firepower—that was it.

This particular instance happened as we were on our way back from an airfield located to the north of Fallujah. As a driver, the two main things I was responsible for while driving was scanning the perimeter for enemy threats and studying the terrain for landmarks and other identifying traits in an effort to become familiar with the area. When we'd made our way to our destination the night before, we were on a route that seemed to take forever due to the bumpy nature of the road and our travels happening at night. We had maps but no experience with that particular area of the country. I remember in particular that when we were at the end of the rough road, we were heading northbound and turned west onto a surface that was much more pleasing. I remember looking off to the east and seeing a bridge going over the road. We turned west at a T, where the bridge was noticed. In my mind, this meant that on the way back, we would be turning south (right) around the time the bridge came into view. Should we come to the bridge, we would know we had gone too far. We made it to the location we intended to go for the night and hunkered down.

Fast forward to the next night—the night of the tenth. We began making our way back to Fallujah after dusk, as night provided a sense of natural cover that we appreciated when possible. I was part of a two-vehicle team that was called the Lead. The two lead vehicles in the convoy were ahead of the rest of the vehicles and tasked with scouting and reporting the coming areas.

Not too long after we were on the road headed back to our base, I saw the bridge from the night before, so I knew our turn south was close. Soon, we were closer than I remembered, so I told my vehicle commander what I was noticing.

"I think we are too close to the bridge, Sergeant."

"Don't worry about it; the staff sergeant knows what he's doing."

"I remember this bridge specifically, and we never came this close."

"Don't worry about it and just keep driving."

I did. Soon we passed under the bridge, which turned out to be an overpass, and came into a small town named Hit. It was quiet—more quiet than usual. There were things we were warned about and told to report if we noticed going on—behaviors and social interactions among Iraqi civilians—because they were cues for hostility. These behaviors were something we all noticed that evening as we drove through that town. As we came to the end of the town, I remember thinking, Whew, *we made it through something I didn't think we were going to.*

Right about that time, I saw a white dog run across the street we were driving on. I told my sergeant, "I will run this dog over before I get off to the side of the road." The insurgents were very good at setting improvised explosive devices (IEDs) just to the side of the road and then setting out decoys and other traps to encourage/entice American troops to veer to the side of the road and into the direct kill zone, or danger area, of the IEDs.

Right about the time I said this, I heard one of the loudest *bangs* I have heard in all my life. It sounded like a firework detonating on the Fourth of July when you are sitting right underneath the display, but much louder. The concussion pounded my chest, and the volume made my left ear ring temporarily. The first thought that came to my mind was, *Why in the world are there kids playing with fireworks in the middle of a combat zone?* That particular thought lasted about one-tenth of one second before I realized our vehicle had just been the target of an IED. In the end, we could only assume the insurgents had planted it just deep enough to fail their desired mission to create casualties—in this case us; we had little damage to our vehicle, and the three of us in the vehicle were unharmed outside of the shock of the concussion, ringing ears, and irritation that somebody had just tried to kill us. The smoke filled the Humvee and was seeping out of the turret where our gunner, Andrew Kamps (a young Marine who would go on to medical school after the war) was using language considered vulgar to even the most seasoned Marine.

As we pushed through the kill zone, several other IEDs exploded on the rest of the platoon behind us and a few Marines witnessed small-arms fire but could not make positive contact to return the favor. After a short distance we noticed headlights and thought it may be an insurgent roadblock, but kept driving. As we approached, we realized it was an Army convoy that had also been hit by an IED while driving the opposite direction, coming toward us. While our multiple-IED attack left our platoon with nothing but minor vehicular damage and no casualties, the Army convoy was not as fortunate in its IED attack. The soldiers were shaken pretty badly, and there were a few of them who were gone. I will never forget the moment my staff sergeant popped open the back of our Humvee, grabbed the body bags we had, and walked off. We set up perimeter security and called for air support and a medical evacuation. After the evacuation took place and we had done all we could, our platoon made our way back to base without further incident.

While I remember the details of the situation vividly, I remember my thoughts more vividly. Most may wonder what they would think in this situation. Some common thoughts are, *I just want to get out of this alive; God, please just let me see my family again; I miss home and don't want to be here.*

While I stood perimeter security and the helicopters came and went out in the middle of the desert in some foreign land, I surrendered my desires for the first time in my life. As I thought about the fact that someone was trying to kill me—not the man in front of or behind me, but me—I had the most gravitating realization I had experienced to that point in my life. It wasn't about me, my children, my friends, or anything except the one thing I found myself whispering aloud: "Lord, I don't know what your plan is, but may it be done. May your will be done." I am as sure of it today as I was on May 10, 2005. This was my first experience ever having the Lord's hand on my shoulder.

* *

The next defining moment would happen a short four months later. After dozens of missions and being hit several more times, we happened to be back on the same bumpy road we'd traveled on in May and on the way to the same airfield. This time I would realize how thin the road was.

As we were heading north on that clear and warm Iraqi September night, we came in contact with yet another Army convoy headed in the opposite direction. As was customary, we attempted to make brief contact, discuss a hasty way to share the road, and be on our way. You don't hang out in Indian Territory for long if it isn't necessary.

At this time in the deployment I was now a sergeant and had been made a vehicle commander of the vehicle that carried our corpsman; our call sign was Red 8. In the sequence of the convoy itself, our vehicle was toward the back for the protection of our corpsman, whom we called Doc.

The convoy came to a stop while the lead vehicles of our convoy made contact with the lead vehicles of the Army convoy we were to pass. As we were stopped, I stepped out to relieve myself of the coffee and water I had been drinking. As I did, I heard what had become the familiar popping sound of an IED. At this point in my deployment, the sound had become recognizable to me, and whether far or close, it was something you just lived with—it was part of the job.

Someone in one of the lead vehicles came over the radio trying to make contact with Red 8, saying there was a need for a medic. The Army convoy's medic wasn't able to move forward to the Army vehicle that had been downed. Being the vehicle commander, I got on the radio and stated that if the vehicles in front of us would make room for us to squeeze forward on the road, we would. They did, and we proceeded forward. We made our way to the front of the Army convoy and soon made visual contact with the downed vehicle.

The first thing I saw when I exited my vehicle were two soldiers, one male and one female, in the road. The male was holding the female, and the female was crying. I asked if they were okay, and the male stated that they were and that the female was just scared. We then moved to the passenger side of the downed vehicle and looked in to see what the situation was.

My eyes were working faster than my brain when I first looked in. I remember the first thought I had was, *Why is this soldier wearing white socks in combat boots? Why are his boots off? Why is his foot in his mouth?* Then, as my brain composed itself and everything registered, I realized that the bottom half of his body was all over the Humvee. As had happened before, the insurgents planted an IED on the side of the road, but because there were two convoys passing and having to share a thin, bumpy road in the dark of night, the insurgents succeeded.

I remember Doc looking at me and saying that while it was pretty much hopeless, we had a job to do. The soldier was still awake, so I talked to him about his deployment and how long his unit had been in country and his family, who was back home waiting for him in Texas. I tried to keep him awake and out of shock. The most amazing thing about that night was that while he was taking what may have been his last breaths of life, he was worried about the other soldiers in his vehicle. Soon, realizing that I could be of more use elsewhere, I left the scene of the Humvee to help another sergeant land the medical evacuation helicopter. We loaded the soldier onto the helicopter, regrouped, and continued our mission.

Because we were the responding vehicle to the downed vehicle, we used our equipment to help the soldier, so it went with him in the helicopter. The next day, our vehicle crew made our way to the airfield hospital where the soldier had been taken to try and retrieve our stretcher. While we were waiting to talk to somebody about retrieving our gear, a helicopter landed. Because they needed help, I assisted in getting off the chopper and into an operating room an Iraqi civilian who had been shot several times along the right side of his body. He screamed the whole time.

As I made my way back to Doc, the surgeon in charge of the airfield hospital arrived. He explained that we could not take the stretcher because the soldier was still on it. That was all that needed to be said. He had not been moved off it onto a hospital bed because he didn't make it.

Looking back, that experience allowed me to gain a lot of insight into mankind and life itself. That night, I saw the best that man had to offer: The idea that somebody who was taking his last breath was more concerned with those around him than he was with himself. The selflessness and love that mankind can have for one another is remarkable, especially with regard to many of our men and women who serve in the United States military. On that same September night, I saw the worst that man has to offer: The fact that there are people who will never meet face to face, who don't know one another's names, but are willing to take the life of that other person in the name of religion, or patriotism, or philosophy.

Allow me to qualify my sentiment by stating that there are things worth fighting for; there are times in which there is no other option but to commit a nation to the horror of war. Ecclesiastes 3 states there is a time for everything, and specifically states there is a time to kill and there is a time for war. I am a firm believer that war should be avoided at all costs and must be a last option. War has been and will continue to be a necessary evil from time to time in the history, both written and not yet written, of the world. That is another lesson I walked away not only from this experience, but the Iraq experience in whole.

The last lesson I learned from this particular experience is the minute role that we as individuals play on this earth. We are here for but the blink of an eye, a shadow of time. What we do with this life affects those around us, and some of us may play a role in shaping something greater, but the size and scope of our roles in the history of man is but a fraction of the blink of an eye.

While this may be the case, that fraction of the blink of that eye and what it represents has meaning, especially to our family, friends, fellow employees, churches, and communities. That lesson brought back from Iraq instilled in me a new spiritual sense—that coming home was my second chance at life and how I affected those around me. Unfortunately, I didn't take that lesson to heed and it cost me greatly, as we will see.

**

It was in 2007 when I made the decision to run for Springfield City Council. I'd returned from Iraq almost two years prior and still had the passion to work for my country. Whether it was at the national level or the local level, I wanted to serve. The decision came with one line that I heard over the airwaves by a talk show host: "You can either complain about what is going on around you or you can do something about it. If you are unsatisfied with what the city council is doing, run against your representative in the next election. You don't have to be somebody that everybody knows or some business owner. You only have to be someone who cares enough to stick their neck out and try your hardest to make a difference." Those were pretty inspiring words to a working-class father, Iraq veteran, and college student.

I started knocking on doors January 2, 2008. I knocked on doors every night after work and as much as my feet could handle and time would allow on Saturdays. I took Wednesdays and Sundays off from knocking. I had a basic message, a lot of passion, and a Marine's discipline and determination. In April of 2009, I won the general election with two-thirds of the vote against the incumbent. I don't attribute my victory entirely to my work ethic and message, but I do feel that those two things carried me past the finish line, which started with the political climate of dissatisfaction and was followed by a lot of support from those family and friends who knew me.

The next two years and eight months were an experience that will be with me for life. When I ran, I spoke about transparency and fiscal accountability. A lot of times, keeping my word landed me in a position in which I was the villain, but there were times when I was the hero, as well. There were times when I felt on top of the world, and there were times when that same world was caving in around me. Further, it was something that often played out in the media—that was the hardest part several times in my time as councilman. The lessons

I learned were many. The first of these lessons was remaining resolute in principle yet flexible in approach.

Another invaluable lesson learned that was largely but not entirely due to my experience on city council was that no matter how much I know about any topic, I am never going to completely understand it—nor is anybody on any topic. An expert is a person who knows much but realizes he doesn't know it all; the person who will admit not knowing but knows just who does or where to find an answer is just as valuable. I learned this in an evolving stage throughout much of my life. It reached the pinnacle right after the New Year of 2012 rang in.

I resigned on the fourth day of January in 2012, immediately following the New Year's Day event that involved me and my estranged wife. I remember writing the letter to Mayor O'Neal. I discussed the fact that I was no longer in a position to effectively represent the constituents, whom I cared for dearly. I talked about the hardships that had plagued me and the recent media spectacles that marked the climax of those events. I remember hitting send on the e-mail that carried the letter as an attached document.

The particular situations will be discussed in short order, but suffice it to say that they were profound enough to cause my resignation.

This, my greatest lesson in humility, brought me to become what is hopefully more compassionate, docile, meek, and contrite than I have ever been before. While this was a defining moment, as was the entire experience, I have come to the firm belief that it was a needed one in order for me to change from who I had become to the man I wanted to be.

**

Soon after my resignation from city council, I remember being approached by many friends who wanted to extend their hands and help in any way they could. In all their efforts, a recurring theme kept popping up. They would ask what kind of general issues I faced in Iraq and if I thought that could be the cause of my behavior. I tried to be as accommodating as possible, but I didn't believe I had experienced enough in Iraq to fall victim to PTSD. Neither did I take into consideration the issues from my childhood or, in particular, my brother's death. While I remained firm in the belief that I didn't have anything wrong with me, I did heed the advice of Cindy, a wonderful friend with whom I served on city council. She told me, "At least give the Veteran's Center a call; just see what they say."

I remember the first time I sat in Ray's room. Ray was my counselor at the Veteran's Center and was a good person for me. He was a counselor, yes, but he was also not afraid to call out my inconsistencies in thought. He let me know right off the bat when a behavior or thought process was not healthy. He was very direct, and that was what I needed. I didn't need any flowery explanations and breathing exercises. I just wanted somebody to shoot it to me straight. Ray was that person for me.

I remember sitting in his office one week while he wanted to discuss my treatment plan. He went over the basic history of the visits we'd had over the past several months. He discussed the issues I brought up: Easily startled, some nightmares, hyper-vigilance, trust issues—those were the main ones, and my emphasis was on hyper-vigilance and trust. I still remember the discussion he and I had about me having a gun at the ready and within five feet of me at all times unless I was at work or somewhere that firearms weren't permitted. I'll never forget him telling me that having it wasn't the issue; the issue was the reason I personally had it.

There we were, rehashing past conversations and discussing the symptoms. Then he read his prognosis. Keeping in mind that he was not a medical doctor and couldn't officially diagnose me, I ended up having the prognosis confirmed by the Veteran's Administration at a later date. He stated that I showed strong symptoms of PTSD caused by both Iraq and childhood experiences, including my brother's death. After that particular meeting, I remember driving home in complete silence. I realized once again the mortality of man, the ability to experience things that affect a man, and that the man in question might not even recognize it. I remember thinking not that I was weak—I didn't think that. I remember thinking not that I needed help—New Year's Day of 2012 made me realize that. What I realized was that I had become a statistic, a man who was affected by the experiences he had in the military and other places, and that I was a part of a community that dealt with something controllable, but medically incurable.

* *

Looking back on the defining moments of my life, I know that we all have those defining moments. Some are more severe than others. Some are good, and some are bad.

I was at a dinner with a friend and we were talking about society as a whole. I discussed my frustration with those in society who make excuses out of their defining moments and then allow the moments that have sculpted them define who they are when they don't succeed. I thought, you know, for all the things I have gone through, I have done okay. I graduated college. I served in the military honorably. I have owned my own home. I have served and worked hard as an elected representative. I never let those moments that could have, with good reason, caused a person to give up to actually allow *me* to give up.

The friend I was at dinner with told me how I was not the "normal" person. He went on to say that many people also go through experiences in life that shape them, but not always with a positive outcome. He didn't make excuses for those who give up and accept the lot they have been given as good reason to accept mediocrity or just getting by; he just made mention that I was different.

I don't see it that way. I had a choice then, and in the more recent situations that have yet to be discussed, I continue to have that choice—free will. I have the choice to fold the hand of cards I've been given and accept what some may call the norms of life, or I can still have dreams, turn them into goals, and work hard to make the goals become reality. I can still work hard to progress emotionally, physically, spiritually, financially, and every other way, or I can say my experiences in life have made me into a person that is only good enough for what he has already accomplished and has in life. In the end, I think I am no different than any other person in this world. I have the same choices that anybody else has who is of sound mind and body. It is what we plan to do through our day-to-day choices that will define and sculpt who we are tomorrow and the day after. Whether it's me, you, the man down the street, or the man in another part of the country, to do anything besides making your dreams become goals and your goals become reality is a disservice to yourself and to your potential.

5.
Sheepdogs

> *"Honor never grows old, and honor rejoices the heart of age. It does so because honor is, finally, about defending those noble and worthy things that deserve defending, even if it comes at a high cost. In our time, that may mean social disapproval, public scorn, hardship, persecution, or as always, even death itself. The question remains: What is worth defending? What is worth dying for? What is worth living for?"*
>
> — *William J. Bennett*

There are many ways one can look at life. There are the optimist and pessimist, the lover and the fighter, the Type A and B personalities. Some of the descriptions deal with how individuals perceive life; some describe how people treat one another; others relate to how people address life. There is another, less known example that describes how people address, perceive, and respond to society. I am not sure where the idea originates, but the first time I came across it was in an e-mail that I received several years back that contained an excerpt of a speech given by a military officer. It was a discussion about wolves, sheep, and sheepdogs.

This description is a categorization that states that all people will fall under one of these three categories. Within these three descriptions, the sheep do not represent the weak or the sheepdogs the strong; rather, the classifications are used to discuss the instinctual nature of the two when confronted with wolves.

The wolf is the predator. He preys on those who appear weak or look vulnerable—the sheep in this metaphor. He is naturally one who has little consideration for others and will do harm to others to achieve some sort of gain for himself. He is aggressive and does not fear the repercussions of his actions. He looks to the sheep as the victims. He comes in many forms. He can be a common thug or criminal, yes, but sometimes he is an individual who seems like nothing more than your average guy, but underneath should be feared.

The wolf preys on the sheep for several reasons. There is nothing wrong with the sheep, and to call this person a sheep is not intended to be derogatory. It is simply stating the fact that he moves through life not as a predator, but also having no idea what to do in the face of a predator. He lives his life, works his job, provides for his family, and enjoys common activities. It is not that he has intentionally chose this way of life per se, but that it has come upon him in the course of life's natural events. His mind is bred for the simple things in life, and he conceives that life is inherently good. He is not used to, nor does he desire confrontation; when faced with it, he is left helpless for his lack of both experience and desire to respond in an equally aggressive manner as the wolf that is accosting him.

Then there is the sheepdog. He is strong like the wolf, but mentally has a very different view of life. He believes that life can be good, which is similar to the sheep, but understands that there are times when situations call for certain individuals to take action and ensure that the goodness of life remains that way. In other words, he believes that the goodness of life is not a given or to be expected, but that there will be times it will be in need of protection and defense.

The sheepdog comes in many forms. He is the police officer; he is the firefighter; he is the emergency responder. He is the soldier, sailor, airman, or marine who signs on a line voluntarily in an effort to protect the values and people that his country stands for. Many times, the public servant takes his uniform off for the last time to rejoin the sheep but has not psychologically reinstated himself into regular society as a former sheepdog...He is still ready to respond as a sheepdog.

Sometimes the sheepdog does not wear a uniform. He is the elected official who is not a politician, but a statesman. He is the guy who will stop what he is doing to help somebody in need even though that somebody is a perfect stranger and in doing so, the sheepdog may be facing danger. He doesn't expect payment, but will take it if being a sheepdog becomes his profession. He never seeks a "thank you," but he is not afraid to look at the person straight-faced and say "you're welcome" because he knows that what he has done is an action above and beyond what most would do. He is a sheepdog not because he does what most wouldn't, but because he does so without second thought, without hesitation, and often times with complete disregard for his safety.

**

As far back as I can remember, I wanted to be in the military. At different periods in my life I also wanted to be a police officer or firefighter. For much of my life I wanted to hold elected office. Regardless of what I wished to do, I never had a burning desire to sit stationary and not make a difference. I have always wanted to make a difference for the betterment of society in a manner that not many other people were willing to pursue.

Two of the goals I had in my youth I was able to complete, and I believe that I did make a difference in those two capacities. I was in the military and I held an elected office. On two very different levels, I was able to change how people lived their lives—in one role, I was helping to offer freedom to the entire nation of Iraq, and in the other, I was helping to form public policy that included public safety, infrastructure, and health.

Arguments can be made as to whether or not I'm a sheepdog, but I would like to hope that in any given situation in which somebody needs help or something needs to be done that not many are willing to offer or do, I will be there. I am compelled to believe that for much of my life, especially since I have been home from Iraq, there have been several times when an opportunity or situation presented itself and I did what I thought was appropriate. Some of those things I have been praised for, some of them I have been called crazy for, and some of them have landed me in the justice system for criminal acts. As for the idea of exposing myself to possible "social disapproval, public scorn, hardship, persecution, or even death itself," those are considerations that have always been secondary. It was not that those considerations have been there and I placed them to the side; rather, those thoughts are not there until after the event and my subsequent actions have taken place. In short, I have always done what I thought to be right in situations in which there was only a split second to take action.

The following experiences, I believe, play a role in the perception one has when considering the legal issues I have faced, why I faced them, and how I played a role. I don't necessarily expect approval or disapproval of the actions I took during the situations I will discuss, but I do hope it gives a more holistic view of the view I had of life and how it has affected me in life.

**

It was a Saturday afternoon and I was on my way back from the gym. I'd had a good workout and looked forward to the rest of the day being a bit more relaxed. I was sitting at an intersection toward the west end of town and waiting on a red light to turn green.

Out of the corner of my eye, I saw a man running out of the front door of an O'Reilly's Auto Store with an employee right behind him. The employee chased him around the side of the building and then gave up on the chase.

At the very moment when the employee gave up the chase, my light turned green. I was able to catch a glimpse of the runner getting into a car that was waiting in an alley behind the store; this was obviously a planned theft. I turned into the alley to immediately get a visual on the car speeding off. I kept some distance but maintained enough speed to keep him in view while he maneuvered through side streets trying to evade me.

There was a split second that he was close enough I could read the license plate. I stopped my pursuit after I wrote the plate number down on a business card.

I returned to the auto store where the situation originated and asked what the scene was about. An employee told me that the thief had grabbed a handful of merchandise and took off on foot out the front door. I gave the employee the card with the plate number and my information and told them that if they needed anything, I would be available. My good deed for the day was done.

* *

The next story is, in my mind, almost silly, so we'll call it the "Office Warrior" story. I was working in the operations department of a law firm at the time. There were two buildings on the same lot, and one day the building I worked in had flowers delivered to it for someone in the second building I was familiar with. I took the delivered flowers across the street to the office of the lady whose name was on the card.

As I walked out of the office, one of the employees who worked in the immediate area said she smelled smoke. I turned and asked her what type of smoke, and she said it smelled like something was burning. At this point, smoke started rising from under her desk. She jumped up and backed away from the computer. Along with the few others who were present, she stood there without taking any action.

My first thought was to get under the desk and unplug everything to prevent a larger electrical fire or the surrounding area itself from catching fire, so that is what I did. As I was under there, I remember thinking, *I'm going to burn the crap out of my hands trying to save what is salvageable.* I remember that as I unplugged the wiring, the flames inside the hard drive were increasing in size. Finally, I was able to unplug the cords and get the computer outside, releasing the employees and building from jeopardy.

Again, the story is borderline silly, but pertinent to understanding the moral of the entirety of this chapter.

* *

Rafael was a short, Mexican kid with curly hair and a little extra weight. He was a good friend of mine when I lived in Long Beach, California. We used to walk to Taco Bell every day after school and hang out there until his father picked him up. After that I would walk home.

On a particular afternoon, we were late getting to Taco Bell. When we came upon the parking lot, his father was there waiting for him. He stepped out of the vehicle, looking angry. Rafael said he had to go and walked away from me. Looking back, as best as my twenty-year memory can serve, I remember him changing his demeanor from the cool and collect kid I knew to somebody who knew there was something negative in store for him.

When he reached his father's car, his father started yelling at him. I couldn't make out what he was saying, but it was aggressive. As Rafael started to get in the car, his father grabbed the back of his head by the hair and began slamming it on the side of the car. After he did this several times, Rafael got in the car and they left.

That night I talked to my father and discussed with him what, if anything, I could do. He gave me several options and, being true to the man my father was, told me it was my decision and that he was sure I would do what was right.

The next day at school I went to the counselor and discussed with her what I'd witnessed. I remember being scared and feeling like I was betraying a friend. It was my first experience in doing what I *believed* was right even when it didn't *feel* right.

I don't remember seeing Rafael again. I am not sure what happened, but I can only hope the best for him, wherever he is. I can also only hope that he and his siblings and possibly mother weren't hurt again. To this day, I hurt when I think of children who are physically abused by a parent—a person whom they depend on for everything, whom they see as larger than life, whom they love and adore and only want to do right by. I have to think that with that in mind, I did what was right.

* *

It was early summer of 2011, and I was on a road trip through the southern end of Missouri. I had stopped at a gas station to pick up a snack in a town named Willow Springs. It was a smaller gas station, and there was only one employee—a middle-aged female.

As I walked in I could sense there was something wrong by the look on the station attendant's face. She carried a look of concern that was easily recognizable, and one that I continued to pay attention to as I casually walked through the store to get what I needed. She continued to be preoccupied with a particular gentleman who was roaming the store. After I finished my shopping, I approached the counter and began to pay. I asked, "Is everything okay?" She responded by telling me she was paying attention to the man roaming around because she'd watched him put several items in his pockets. A younger, possibly college-aged kid in line behind me was paying attention to the conversation even though we were speaking at a low volume. I asked if the attendant felt she needed help; she responded not by saying yes, but by stating she didn't know what to do. (Considering the circumstances, I'm sure she didn't want to be held liable if something happened and someone was injured.)

I stepped away from the counter and approached the man. I noticed in my peripheral vision that the young man behind me in line was watching attentively. I walked up to the gentleman and said, "How are you today?" He just looked at me, so I continued. "Look, I don't want to cause any trouble, but the lady behind the counter sees what you're doing and just wants you to put the stuff back and leave." He said, "I don't know what you're talking about." I responded, "The lady has no reason to simply make this up. You need to put the stuff in your pockets back and leave the store."

At this point he squared off as if ready to get into a physical altercation. He was a man of small stature, but so was I. I didn't believe him to be much of a threat, but I saw it as reasonable that he would view me the same way. "What are you going to do," he asked.

"Alright, I am trying to help the lady out and you just need to put the merchandise back and leave. Nobody wants any trouble." At this time, the young man left his place in line and partially made his way to where I was standing. I continued. "I understand the position you're in, but the fact is that you are not leaving until you put the stuff in your pockets back. Nobody wants to call the police, and nobody wants trouble. We're just asking you to do what is right." He asked at that point, "Who's going to stop me?" I responded, "There are two people standing right here that are probably going to make sure you don't steal from this store." I indicated myself and the young man who, at this point, was clearly there in support. The shoplifter stood stationary for about ten seconds, looking straight at me. After that short period of time, he took several items, mostly candy, out of his pocket, set them down, and walked out of the store.

The man was a thief, the clerk didn't know what to do, and me doing something to help seemed like a few minutes of my time and not that big of a deal—those things are clear. What isn't clear is whether or not five to ten dollars' worth of merchandise is worth a physical altercation. The decision I made was not based on the monetary value, because I didn't see any in that instant; what I saw was a lady who was concerned that her business/place of employment was going to lose money due to the disrespectful nature of a shoplifter. I chose to help the lady; she was appreciative of that. I can't say that I would do anything different if put in that situation again.

* *

In June of either 2008 or 2009 (the exact year evades me, but the date was the twenty-sixth), I was working as a sales representative for an industrial products company in Springfield, Missouri, as I was for most of my stories that take place in Springfield. I had made a delivery of some goods and was on my way back to the office from the customer's place of business in the company vehicle, facing east, and the first car at the light in the left-hand turn lane. I was stopped, as the green light was for the north/south traffic. I noticed a north-facing vehicle try to make a left turn and saw hesitation in the movement of the car before it proceeded to go for the left turn. As this happened, a southbound car going at the regular rate of speed (forty to fifty miles per hour) T-boned the car turning left. I remember thinking to myself in that split second how amazing it was to me that a small sports sedan could T-bone a larger Lincoln Town Car and actually catapult it into the air and upside down, leaving the small sports sedan immediately stationary after impact.

The next thing I remember thinking was that the Lincoln, in the air and flipping upside down, was headed in my direction. When the vehicle landed, it did so about ten feet in front of me.

I reacted psychologically as I would have in Iraq; my first response was, "Well, there are people that are in trouble, so let me see how I can help." I immediately exited the company vehicle and went to the upside-down car. I could see that there were three people in the vehicle. The driver, an older male, was injured but conscious, as was the passenger, a woman in her mid-forties or early fifties, but the lady in the back seat, an elderly woman, was unconscious. The lady in the passenger seat was screaming for somebody to help her, and the other two were silent.

Luckily, an ambulance happened to be nearby and stopped at the scene. The obvious need was with those in the car that was upside down, and that is where the EMTs concentrated their efforts. As this was unfolding, I walked over to the small sports sedan. The driver was the only individual in the car. She was conscious but visibly distraught. I talked with her for a minute, ensured she was not in shock, and asked her if there was anything I could do. She responded in a manner letting me know she was fine, just scared.

I went back over to see if there was anything I could do to help the EMTs, and they let me know there was nothing they could physically do until the fire department arrived because the car had the passengers trapped. One of the EMTs did ask that I keep the driver awake, as he had a contusion on his head and possibly a brain injury. I did as he asked until there was enough medical support on the scene.

This is not some heroic story, nor is it a story that shows I did something spectacular. I did what I could in a situation in which there were people hurt and there was a high level of anxiety. The story is not about me, but it is also not about the EMTs, police on the scene, injured people involved, or the fire department with the tools to extract the victims. It is a reflection of the fact that in a time of immediate reaction and in busy traffic, two people who weren't first responders stopped—me and one other person. That other person stood on the sidewalk and watched until it was time to give his story to the police. All other drivers who saw what happened at the stoplight drove by. Would they have driven by if a body had been ejected? Would they have driven by if one of the cars was on fire? I don't know the answer, but I do know that they didn't stop when they were in no danger post-accident and, from the appearance of the accident, other people were.

Concerning the accident's involved parties, they all made recoveries. Some had minor injuries and others had more serious, but not life-threatening injuries.

I didn't feel as if I did anything particularly special; I made an assessment of the situation that I could relay to the medical responders and helped keep one man out of shock. Later I was called as a witness and was given an exceedingly grateful "thank you" by the lady in the sports sedan. Several times after that, we met in passing around town by happenstance, and each time she made it known that I'd made her feel safe, that I was there and had comforted her in a time of great anxiety and fear. That alone made me feel like I'd done something good, though I don't know that I really did anything at all.

* *

It seemed like just another day—I don't even remember the day of the week. I had just gotten off work and decided to stop at the local gas station to pick some things up on my way home. The store was close enough to home that I knew the employees and they knew me, so as I was paying, the clerks and I were chatting about the day's events. All of a sudden one of the two clerks shouted, "He's stealing gas!"

I turned from the cash register as the second clerk handed me the receipt for my purchase and saw a vehicle speeding off the gas station lot. At that split second, and without second thought, I hurried to my car, started it, and took off through the parking lot in the same direction as the gas thief.

The intersection where the gas station was located was a busy one during the afternoon rush hour, and I was aware of this. I got to the exit of the lot, which was at the northwest corner of the intersection, noted that the route for me to make my way across the intersection was relatively safe, and took the opportunity. The vehicle was headed south, so the pass-through traffic was not kitty-corner, only north to south. Because several lanes (two for the left turn, two going straight, and one for the right turn) were busy, I was forced to take the shoulder of the road to keep the thief in sight and range. Within a few seconds of me being at the cash register, I was now behind the thief, across the intersection, and following him with confidence.

During the initial part of the pursuit I dialed 911. I had the operator on the phone for the majority of the pursuit and discussed the make, model, and plate number of the car while I was following him on the main road. As we got to the next main intersection, approximately a mile or two down the road, his vehicle started to give out—it was a later model vehicle and didn't seem to be maintained properly. At this time in my life, I carried a gun with me in the side pocket of my door; I'd carried one in that same place since I returned from Iraq in late 2005. This was one of the few times I thought I may have to use it.

The man driving the vehicle pulled onto the median in the middle of the road and stepped out. At this point I was pretty confident he knew I was following him, so I gave the dispatcher his description as I pulled over behind his vehicle at a little distance and on the median. He walked to the rear of his vehicle and looked around before he grabbed a gas can and walked across the two eastbound lanes of the expressway. There was a Wal-Mart, a gas station, and a few other smaller stores, which made where he headed highly populated. Because of this, I asked the dispatcher if I should follow him; while I was waiting for her response, I began to pull forward and around the broken-down car to be able to drive into the parking lot in case her response was yes.

As I pulled in front of the car but still on the median, the dispatcher told me to stay where I was and keep an eye on the car. A couple of minutes passed and the driver reappeared wearing different clothes. I saw that he was going to his vehicle but clearly looking in the direction of my car. At this point, because I didn't know what he was thinking, I readied my Glock 9mm to fire with a round in the chamber. I explained to the 911 dispatcher that something was clearly going to happen if the police weren't near.

At this exact moment, a squad car arrived. One of the officers immediately detained the driver of the vehicle for stealing the gas. The other officer, Officer Steele, took my information and story. This would not be the last time I met Officer Steele while he was in the field, but it would be the last time I met him under favorable conditions.

It turned out that the perpetrator had taken almost $100 in gas. I returned to the gas station to let them know the police had detained the thief and to give them the report number I was given. I walked away from that experience feeling it had been a little risky, but I had done something good for the community in a small way.

**

In these experiences, I was in a place and situation by happenstance and conducted myself the best I knew how. When I told these stories to friends or family, I got mixed reactions. When people gave a more negative reaction, I asked them how many more times the thief would have shoplifted or stolen gas. What if the computer fire had led to a structural fire? Would anybody else have turned in the abusive father had I not been there? Then I always give two extreme stories—not because I believe that I saved something from happening under similar circumstances, but to express and give an example of what can happen when people do nothing.

**

Not far from where I used to live on the west side of town, there was a murder/suicide that took place inside a home; the couple who lived there were the victims. The husband murdered his wife and then committed suicide. The couple had had issues with the law regarding domestic abuse in the past, and the husband had been in trouble because of it. When the investigation of the deaths took place, the police found two instances in which somebody could have simply made a phone call to the police and quite possibly prevented the deaths from occurring. The first was when a neighbor reported he'd heard a bad verbal confrontation; the second was a neighbor who saw the wife run from the house and the husband run after her with a knife; after he caught her, the neighbor saw him drag her back in the home. What could have possibly been the reason nobody did anything? Was it "not their business" or was "somebody else going to take care of it"? The answer doesn't matter. What does matter, as I was told by a veteran police officer, is that the end result was more than likely avoidable.

**

The second instance also took place near my former residence. On the way to work, I remember hearing a reporter on the radio mentioning a murder that took place in the parking lot of a fast food restaurant near the same location the gas thief stole the gas in my previous story.

As the reports came through, the story discussed an estranged husband and wife who were in the same car and driving around in the area. In the end, they parked in the restaurant parking lot, where the husband stabbed the wife to death.

When follow-up reports came, there were statements made by witnesses who saw the car swerving in and out of traffic and who saw the direction the man took as he exited the car. When the witnesses paid this much attention and knew this much detail, that leads me to believe they knew something was not right.

Who could have stopped what happened from happening? I don't know if anybody could have, nor do I know if anybody attempting to do something would have created more than one victim. The point is that nobody did anything, and we'll never know the answer. What we do know is that while a woman was being murdered in broad daylight and the perpetrator walked freely away (though I do believe he was later apprehended), people who were in the area did nothing. "It wasn't their business."

* *

The previous stories are ones I believe necessary to set the stage for the next chapter. They are not stories meant to revel in my actions or attempt to make myself out to be something I'm not. I am a guy who was trained in the military to take care of issues as they arise and to not be afraid to do what is right even when it is uncomfortable or when consequences may result. I wanted to set the next chapter up by discussing these previous experiences to help you understand that what happened on Thanksgiving Day of 2011 started as nothing out of the ordinary given the circumstances. It was something that began as just another action I took in an effort to do what I perceived was right—as it turns out, this was my lesson in how good intentions can go awry.

6.
The Memorable Thanksgiving

The following is the story of what happened on Thanksgiving Day of 2011—the beginning of the turn of events that would eventually lead to my resignation from Springfield City Council. I believe it is necessary to preface this chapter by stating a few facts. I have written this chapter to explain the situation as I remember it cognitively, and I use the police reports as a tool to help guide the story. I am not making excuses, nor am I admitting that I believe any person to be any more guilty or innocent than what the reader himself concludes. This is simply the side of the story that was not allowed in the media for many months due to the investigation of and trial for my actions. I needed to remain silent for my legal safety. Again, what follows is my story.

The story is primarily taken from the police report and includes two different statements, unabridged for clarity. What I stated to the police is what I stand by as having happened, as it is the truth. Throughout the first portion of the chapter, the italicized text is that of my personal explanation and is not part of the police reports.

**

First Account:

"On 11/24/11 at 1544 hours [police officer] responded to [address] to contact male, Nicholas Ibarra, who had possibly been involved in an accident and assault at [location of incident]. Upon my arrival to the address a male I recognized as Nicholas Ibarra was standing on the front porch of the address. Ibarra had called into dispatch requesting to speak with officers at the address in reference to the incident on [address].

"[Police officer] also responded to the address and we contacted Ibarra on the front porch of the address. I immediately noted Ibarra's eyes were watery. We informed Ibarra we were at the address to attempt and receive a statement from him about the incident that occurred on [address]. Ibarra agreed to speak with me about the incident. As Ibarra began to speak I noted a strong odor of intoxicants coming from person. The odor appeared to get stronger as Ibarra spoke. I was standing about three feet in front of Ibarra as I spoke with him."

Throughout the day, I'd had a couple of alcoholic beverages only. I refrained toward the afternoon because I was leaving to see my children. After the incident occurred, I went back to my mother's house, where I had been a majority of that afternoon, and had several drinks while waiting for the police to arrive. This admission was later noted in the report.

"Ibarra began to speak rapidly giving his statement about what had occurred. According to Ibarra, he was going home when another male 'cut him off' on Grand St. He responded by cutting the male off with his vehicle. He followed the male and when the male he was following stopped at a stoplight Ibarra got out of his vehicle and asked the juvenile what his problem was. The male told Ibarra he needed to talk to his Dad if he wanted to speak with someone."

The cutting back and forth with the other car on the road went from the center of town to the west end of town. At this point, I thought, Okay, if this kid was mine, I would want to know he was driving in such a manner. What I didn't consider was that the juvenile had the whole way home to get on the phone with his father and tell him anything he wanted about the situation, regardless of what the truth was.

"Ibarra stated he followed the juvenile male to an address on [address]. He stopped and got out of his vehicle. Several members of what Ibarra believed were family members of the juvenile male were in the yard of the address as he stopped. Several persons, including an older male began to come toward him. Ibarra began handing out business cards to several of the persons in the roadway. He gave the older male a business card and began talking to him about the juvenile male cutting him off. At that time an unknown person who was in the street next to him struck Ibarra in his left ear."

The intent of handing out business cards was to let them know that I was a councilman. I didn't mean any disrespect, and I wasn't some guy picking a fight in traffic—I meant well.

"Ibarra then got in to his car and another male began reaching in to his vehicle through the window. The male was asking him, 'Are you drunk?' The male told Ibarra, 'You can't start your car' and telling Ibarra he couldn't leave. As the male began climbing into Ibarra's vehicle, Ibarra began backing the vehicle. While backing the vehicle he struck a mailbox. The male 'kid' wouldn't get out of his (Ibarra's) car.

"Ibarra then stated, 'I guess I reverted back to Iraq. I did have a gun. They didn't have a gun so that wasn't the answer. Ibarra continued and stated once the male 'got out of the car' Ibarra backed up to Mt. Vernon St. 'squared away' and left.

"[Police officer] interjected and informed Ibarra that he had an odor of intoxicants coming from his person. [Police officer] asked Ibarra if he would submit to a PBT breath test. Ibarra claimed he had not been drinking prior to the incident. Ibarra stated, 'I came back here and my step dad got me drunk.' Ibarra made this statement at 1602 hours."

As I contested then, the incident happened at minimum an hour before they'd arrived to take my statement. When I arrived back at my mother's home, I drank several glasses of brandy, and I drank it straight. As I will mention later, the difference in my demeanor at the time of my statement and at the time of the incident is very noticeable.

"Ibarra then contacted someone on his cell phone. Ibarra claimed it was his lawyer and wanted his/her opinion before submitting to a PBT. Ibarra agreed to submit to the PBT after hanging up his cell phone.

"Ibarra then asked to contact his family inside the address. He opened the door to the address and had his uncle, [name], his stepfather, [name], and his mother, [name], exit the address onto the front porch. Ibarra asked the three family members if he had been drinking since he arrived at [address]. They all responded affirmatively.

"[Uncle] and [step-father] stated [uncle] had told Ibarra to come inside and have a drink of brandy. [Step-father] stated Ibarra arrived at the address and was frantic.

"After Ibarra submitted to a PBT Ibarra agreed to give me his account of the incident with further detail since his original statement was rapid and not complete.

Second Account:

"According to Ibarra, he was driving west on Grand, somewhere between Scenic and West Bypass. A younger male driving a vehicle 'cut him off' and then he in turn 'cut him off.' Ibarra stated, 'I was in the wrong.' Ibarra described the driver of the other vehicle as a younger possibly 16 or 17 year old white/male. Ibarra stated, 'I was a prick.' The younger male, passed him again on Grand and Ibarra followed the male in his vehicle. The male took a right (north) on W. Bypass from Grand[,] the male approached Mt. Vernon St. and took a right (east). Ibarra was continuing to follow the male. The male then took a right (south) on Western Ave. and as Ibarra followed him the male made a U-turn on Western and then went left (west) on Mt. Vernon. Ibarra stated he followed the male. The male was stopped at the red light Mt. Vernon/W. Bypass (facing east). Ibarra pulled his vehicle behind the male's and exited his vehicle. He contacted the male who was seated in his respective vehicle's driver's seat. Ibarra believed the male was alone in the vehicle. He asked the male, "What's your problem?" The male responded telling Ibarra if he had a problem to talk to his Dad. Ibarra agreed to speak with the 'Dad' and followed the male to an address on [street name].

"Once at the address on [street name] Ibarra stopped his vehicle in the street behind the male who had pulled into a driveway. Ibarra exited his vehicle. An older male was in the roadway already and Ibarra spoke to the older male for '1/2 second.' Ibarra stated the older male was a white/male in his 50's about 5'10" 130lbs. Ibarra had no further description of the older male. As he began speaking with the older male he gave him a business card. There were about five other 17 to 21 year old white/males in the roadway. Ibarra stated he never left the doorway of his vehicle and was always within arms length of his car. One of the unknown younger males then struck Ibarra in the left ear with something. Ibarra was unsure if it was a male striking him with a fist or something else. Ibarra did not know who had struck him. Ibarra couldn't give a better description of the males in the roadway.

"Ibarra got into his vehicle and one of the males in the street leaned into his drivers side window. The male stated, 'I think you've been drinking Mr. Ibarra.' The male then tried to keep him from putting his keys in the ignition or putting his vehicle in gear. The male had half of his body in the car as Ibarra began backing down [street name]. Ibarra stated, 'You and your friend are trying to jack me.' The male was hanging in the vehicle as Ibarra continued to back up. The male was stating, 'You hurting me Mr. Ibarra.' Ibarra stated he was 'afraid.' As the vehicle continued to back up the male fell from the vehicle in the roadway. Ibarra didn't see the male after he fell from the vehicle. Ibarra believed he struck a mailbox before backing to Mt. Vernon and then proceeding east on Mt. Vernon."

**

The statement I gave, which was entered in the report, and the events surrounding that statement go on to discuss that I waited to get to my mother's to call the police. I never stated to the police that I waited until then to call, and that part of the report is inaccurate. I called the police on the way back to my mother's. I did make one phone call before that. I called the kids' mother to let her know what happened since she was bringing the kids to see me; immediately after that, I called 911.

The report also goes on to state that pictures were taken. One in particular showed my sunroof and its damage. The report states that I "was unsure" about how the damage happened. The issue with this is that I wasn't unsure. In context, the police officer asked me if I knew how it happened; I did my best to explain that the damage wasn't there before the incident, but it was there immediately following the incident. While I didn't physically witness the damage being done, I knew how and when it was done. Maybe I should have been more direct.

Lastly, there is a portion of the report that discusses the police asking for permission to go through my car to look for a cell phone belonging to one of the men who were climbing into my car. I searched first, and I did find an empty 50ml bottle of liquor that had been in my side compartment—a place I stored other trash, as well. I attempted to conceal it, and the officer saw and seized the container.

**

As I write this chapter, I am still awaiting trial for that day. I was charged with three counts of felony assault and one count of tampering with evidence. As I read the report the first time I was, quite frankly, sick to my stomach. Along with the simple fact that I was reading the story that forever changed my life and that of my children and friends, I also came across many issues in the report that seem to have been overlooked.

**

During the investigation, several people were interviewed on both the side of the other party and my side. While the complete 200+ page report is public, I do want to review some things that are in the report and that I believe to be of great importance. Though the issues discussed are taken objectively from the report, do understand that the words below are mine and are subjectively written from my point of view.

**

One of the first things I noticed in the report that didn't make logical sense to me was in regard to the stories of the other parties directly involved. It was said that I held the man in my car on purpose. It was stated that I held him chicken-wing style while I was driving off. What concerns me about the accusation is that I supposedly dragged a man for what was measured at almost 700 feet—more than 2 football fields—with the following factors: I was doing so at a "high speed" and *in reverse*, holding onto somebody with one arm (presumably my left) and steering with my right hand, on a road that had several cars parked up and down the street—it was Thanksgiving, after all. Now, while I may have driven the streets of Iraq for a tour of duty, I will say that what they claimed I did was pretty spectacular. In the end, if their claims that I seemed intoxicated were true, which we will discuss shortly, I did all of this, and successfully so, while looking in my rearview mirror. Not to demean myself, but that much talent is not inherent in one Mr. Nicholas B. Ibarra.

When the responding officers asked to interview the person with whom I'd had the original altercation on the road, one of the eye witnesses specifically stated to the police that she knew he had a felony warrant out for his arrest and that was why he left before the police arrived. While the felony didn't have anything to do directly with the situation at hand, I do believe it speaks to the character of those involved in the altercation because they knew about the felony warrant and let the person leave the scene of a major incident.

During the interview process, one of the police officers reported, "I asked [name] what caused him to believe [Ibarra had been drinking]. [Name] told me it was Ibarra's demeanor that caused him to believe this. It was his assumption that he had the authority to control the situation. [Name] said he could smell beer on Ibarra's breath but he did not stagger when he walked. His speech was not slurred."

My response is simple. I was trying to do what I thought was right in correcting a situation in which somebody was acting inappropriately. When I arrived at the house I was led to, I was soon surrounded by a semi-circle made up of several males. Being a Marine sergeant who has a fairly good sense of when situations are possibly hostile, I can assure you that *was* the atmosphere of that moment. In my mind, I had two choices—to act timid or to be sure of myself and confident in my approach. I chose the latter of the two.

Looking back, I must admit that I don't remember saying this to the people who claim I did, but along with the reporting officer, both the Springfield city manager (with whom I spoke) and my stepfather made references to me either mentioning Iraq or having behaviors representing my experience in Iraq.

Further in the interview of one of the two injured individuals, the interviewee specifically stated *he grabbed the car to avoid falling when the car started moving.* He then recanted an earlier statement in which he claimed I held his shirt. The individual later stated his memory was bad, which was seemingly why he couldn't remember, but the report notes that until he was struck by the mailbox that I hit with the car, he was very clear as to what happened. When the mailbox was hit, the person hanging in my car fell off—supposedly at impact. Considering the charges that were filed against me, I personally believe this part of the "victim's" statement to be of interest. If, in fact, he both grabbed the car and recanted the statement that I grabbed him to hold him in my car intentionally, does that not change the atmosphere and the scenario of the entire situation? I know that my opinion is a subjective and biased one, so I'll leave the reader to be the judge.

The last item in the report was a statement taken from one of the family members of the victim who was not in the street, but in the yard of the property owner the other parties involved were visiting. Her statement was important because those involved in the actual altercation stated time and again that there was no assault that took place during the conversation on the street. The witness, a member of that same party, stated specifically that she saw physical aggression, but she wasn't sure between whom. She did say at the time she thought it was between me and the other driver, but wasn't sure about that or who was aggressive toward who.

**

As a child, I was always taught to stand up for what I believe in, to stand my ground, and to look difficult times in the face. This was the first experience I had in life when I was not able to do that. I was not able to defend myself against the accusations. I was not allowed to make a public comment. I was not allowed to explain my side of the story.

I understand that the reason for not being able to do so was my protection and that the advice given to me by Tyson, my lawyer, was advice I knew would come and knew would remain. That put me in a position of watching a "media trial" go on without a key witness there to, at minimum, give his version of the story. This was one of those times I felt as if the world was crashing down on me.

Though I am only sitting and writing this story right now, I know in time the sense of relief I will feel to know that good or bad, right or wrong, my story is told will be immense. As I consider the issue even further, I hope all parties involved are willing to allow the police report *in whole* (including the medical reports) to be released, and those so interested in telling one side of the story will be honest enough to tell the other side, as well.

As stated before, I do not wish to lay blame on anybody but those who are responsible. I plan to pay the price given to me for what the justice system deems I have done. I plan to take responsibility and accept the punishment for the actions I have taken—but nothing more. I plan to be open about my experience when the time comes.

Looking back, were there things I would have done differently? Hindsight says yes, but to consider the actions I took and cannot change does little good. What I do know is this: I believe the occasions of both Thanksgiving and the New Year's that followed are two occasions that nature afforded me to realize I needed a different path in life if I hoped to have children that loved their father, to see my later years, and to do so as a free individual who could have a second (okay, third) chance at life for his remaining years. I intend to make those things happen with nothing but love for my ambitions that can still be realized, love for my family and friends who stood beside me in my darkest hour, and a love of life that wouldn't have been realized had I not been through the gauntlet presented to me in the later part of the year 2011.

7.
Trial by Media

It is interesting the way the human mind works—the *idea* of a person's frame of reference is astonishing. You often hear (and depending on your age, you may feel) that the longer you live, the shorter the years get. I liken it to two different types of people who read books. The first, the long-winded reader, commonly reads books of 700 pages or more. The second, the short-winded reader, reads 300-page books. When both are presented with a 500-page book, the long-winded reader sees a small book, whereas the short-winded reader sees a large book. The same goes for life beyond birthdays and years on this earth. It goes to say that through our experiences in life, we learn and often have to adapt and overcome. As those experiences happen, they shape our own, individual perceptions.

The life of someone commonly subjected to media coverage is no different. As somebody running for Springfield City Council, I was excited to see my name in the paper or on the news in the beginning. I was fascinated not by being on television or in print, but by the idea that people were asking my opinion on pertinent issues that faced the community. It made me feel as if my voice was being heard, and when I won my election sixty-eight percent to thirty-two percent over a two-term incumbent, it let me know that what I hoped to offer the community was something that they agreed with to an extent large enough to vote for me.

Then time passed, and being recognized became something of the norm. I would always feel good greeting people in public who would let me know they approved of my work, but I also appreciated those who would challenge me. In being challenged by constituents, I was forced to constantly evaluate my values, votes, and positions. It was a good thing in my eyes.

As can be assumed, being somebody who ran for elected office on the idea of changing the outlook of government and asking to be elected because I wasn't the "same-ole, same-ole," there were positions I took that were very controversial at the municipal level of government; that attracted a fair amount of media attention. Knowing this was going to be the case from the beginning, I had a motto: The media is going to be there; you have the choice to make them your best friend or your worst enemy, but the choice is up to you. I chose to work with them as much as possible. I never refused an interview unless I was simply not available, and I never skirted or refused to answer questions. They may not have been my best friends, but I never believed I was treated unfairly, taken out of context, or given criticism save in one instance while serving as a councilman. Not until the end did I ever consider the media to *not* be an ally via fair coverage.

As discussed a short time ago, however, experience changes perspective. I remember the day of the "road rage" occurrence (so named by the media) on Thanksgiving Day of 2011 and how the days that proceeded were a valuable lesson in how the media reports. Coupled with the incident itself, I hope the discussion in the chapter "Sheepdogs" has given light to how accurate the given title "road rage" was regarding what I was doing on Thanksgiving.

As for the topic at hand, I want to discuss the way the media addresses issues when they occur. The difficult part about writing this chapter is that I'm still in the mindset that the media is an omnipotent entity that has the ability to persuade the thoughts of the public. As a former office holder, I hold close to the idea that what I do and say is going to be scrutinized regardless of how I approach an issue. In short, it's hard to be objective, but I have to come to accept that the media is going to be harsh if that's what it takes to sell, regardless of whom they affect and how inefficient the reporting is. Whether it's local or national media, it is the same. Different outlets are going to report on the same issues, but there is a slant that alludes to each media company's bias. Whether the issue is government actions, social issues, or economic issues, it is not hard to find bias in most media reporting.

I remember that when I was serving with the Marines in Iraq in 2005, we would get the opportunity to eat at a chow hall regularly, and that chow hall always had a major national news source playing on several televisions located in several places in the small building. I specifically remember that the interpretation of what was going on "on the ground" in Iraq on these stations was so terribly different from what was really going on in the eyes of those on the ground.

Local media reporting local issues is no different. I understand media is a business and, as such, has an obligation to report stories that people are interested in. At the same time, I do feel the reporting was overdone regarding the Thanksgiving Day incident when my home address was posted and my Social Security number was made public. There were also other personal issues about family members who weren't involved in the situation but were put on public display.

In the beginning I didn't see the overbearing manner of the reporting. While I felt completely sick to my stomach, had anxiety attacks for days, and couldn't function psychologically due to the internal pressure of what was going on, I recognized and acknowledged that this was something that was going to be reported on and that there was nothing I could do about it.

Within a few days, I did notice that television media was replaying the same broadcast day after day for about a week; there was nothing new to report. I also noticed the print media would copy and paste the same article, then add some sort of different twist to make it a "new" story. They did so for *over* a week. I simply thought that this was the way the news cycle was going and didn't think differently until much of the public started scrutinizing some of the media outlets to the point that the print media had to print an opinion piece defending their actions. After that, the reporting died down; I am still curious about whether it was because they realized fault or because it wasn't a seller any longer.

Backing up a little and looking at the micro rather than the macro, I remember when the Thanksgiving Day incident began to be reported by the media. Before the first story ran, I remember getting a call from the newspaper telling me they were going to post the story on the Internet and that they wanted to let me know. I can't say that I was upset by the article, but what was astounding was the immediate vitriol displayed by anonymous commenters who could post their thoughts at the end of the story. It was in every sense a trial by media and by a group of individuals who didn't have to account for their statements because of the anonymous nature of the commenting on the web sites.

Then came the individuals with whom the altercation occurred. When the situation happened, I gave them my business card and explained who I was in an effort to diffuse the confrontational attitude with which I was initially approached. After the smoke settled from the incident itself, those I'd had the altercation with immediately contacted the media because, to paraphrase, they were concerned I'd tried to kill them and wasn't in jail. Well, the media ate that up and gave them their fifteen minutes of fame. They were portrayed as poor victims assaulted by an elected official who thought he could "do whatever he wanted."

It was a short time later that another altercation happened, this time with my now ex-wife. It happened on New Year's Day, and again the police were involved. I was arrested and charged with Unlawful Use of a Weapon. Again, the commenters were out in full force. Without knowing anything but the media's 2-minute segment or 500-word article, I was immediately labeled as an abusive husband who needed to be investigated for everything imaginable, including child abuse. The severity with which people in my very own community would make judgment calls on something about which there was little information available was astounding.

Whether it was through my time on city council or the time leading up to my resignation during the first week of January, I have gained what I believe to be a very intricate perspective of the way the media operates and how they are at times unwavering, regardless of whom they are hurting or what they are damaging. I have seen both the side of the viewer and the story participant in a very in-depth way.

As stated before, I don't hold a grudge against the media. If there is anything to forgive, I do. They were hopefully doing their job in the way they believed was the best for the communities they served; my sadness comes with the idea of the lives of people often being affected for the worse when certain things are reported in a manner that is meant to boost ratings rather than provide information and truth. That is a key lesson I will take with me through life when considering what's reported nationally, internationally, and locally and how I perceive a story.

8.
Over the Edge

When I was in the Marines during my initial enlistment, the corps was offering re-enlistment bonuses and options to go to a specialized school such as jump school, where you learn to jump out of planes, or scuba school for underwater military divers. One of the schools, though—the one that I would have picked—was S.E.R.E. School. The acronym stands for Survival, Evasion, Resistance, and Escape.

There are different programs in S.E.R.E.; the more advanced program may not have been what I would have participated in, but is one that is pertinent to this chapter. In the more advanced program, one of the primary focuses is the student at a higher risk of being captured by enemy forces, so the school hones in on the topics of resistance and escape. Resistance means to withstand or to be able to endure something or someone who is creating a negative force. I don't know much about the program itself, but thinking about what must go on leads me to think there is a practical application portion of the program that involves seeing just how much a student can withstand physically, mentally, and emotionally.

The correlation here is with life itself. I lived much of my life—the deaths of my family members, moving around from location to location, being somewhat on my own from the time I was thirteen, Iraq, etc.—believing that I could endure the issues I faced and the hardships I experienced. I believed that I could continue on regardless of what was going on inside and not have a climactic set of events completely alter my life. It was on New Year's Day of 2012 that my mind changed.

While I am going to discuss the details of what happened, I am going to omit names for the purposes of the privacy of those involved and of those I love who may not have had a direct role in what happened but were impacted just the same. The purpose of me sharing this story is to discuss the fact that there are men and women, many of whom have served in the military, who have things inside their hearts and minds that they don't share. They perceive the problem to be a problem of weakness; they have been trained to remain solid, to not reveal any sort of weakness or flaw. This story is to share not only the fact that I had that exact problem, but that my blindness to it refused to let me see the worst thing of all, that it was allowing myself, my family, my friends, and, in the end, my constituents to suffer. It is to also discuss an example of what happens when those problems fester and build to the point that one goes over the edge.

**

I woke up excited. It was New Year's Day of 2012; there was nothing but hope and light ahead for the next 365 days. I was excited about the Presidential election; I was excited about being on city council and "fighting the good fight" on local issues; I was starting a new personal life and moving beyond what had been a difficult twelve years of marriage. Things were good on the surface.

I had stayed the night with a friend the night before and was given a ride to the house I was staying at for the time being. I refer to this particular house as such because while it was the house I had bought and lived in for six years, I was only staying there temporarily while my estranged wife was supposed to be staying with her parents…While that was the agreement, it was a regular thing for her to come to the house and get stuff or do stuff.

This particular morning started off with me deciding to drink alcohol. I had not imbibed except on two occasions since the Thanksgiving Day altercation with constituents: I had several drinks the night before, which was New Year's Eve, and a couple of drinks on Christmas Day.

This particular day, January first, I decided to go all out. Beer and wine was my choice, so I bought enough to get me through the day and rented a few movies.

This decision was due in part to the fact that I was under the impression that my kids were with friends and that my daughter would be picked up by her mother. When I tried to contact her mother to confirm this fact, I was ignored at first. (This was not a cordial relationship, to say the least.) When she finally did respond, a verbal and phone text altercation started. What frustrated me was that, from the best of my recollection, I could not get her to simply answer what was going on with my daughter (what friend's she was at, did she still have a ride, etc.).

As the altercation escalated, so did my frustration. My anger swelled to the point that I began making threats. I sincerely don't remember exactly how the conversation progressed, but it did get to a point that I threatened to kill her and myself. I also remember getting my Glock 9mm from my car and laying the clip, bullets, and gun all out on the coffee table in the living room.

Eventually, not taking my threats seriously, my estranged wife showed up claiming she was going to take a shower, get clothes, and leave. This was not outside of the ordinary, but this made me even more enraged. She wasn't taking me seriously. She wasn't taking my threats seriously. Further, her attitude was one that, at the time, I thought was condescending and extremely rude.

It was at this point I thought, *I am so mad right now. I am so mad and angry and enraged, and she doesn't get it. I want her to feel as much fear as I feel anger—and I want her to feel it right now.*

I took my gun and loaded it; I put a round in the chamber, and I walked into the bathroom where she was standing. I pointed the gun at her and began to yell. I don't remember ever thinking I was going to shoot her, but I do remember thinking how much I hurt, how bad the pain was, and how tired I was. I was tired of the darkness I felt in my heart no matter how many positive things there were on the outside. I was tired of pretending everything was alright when it wasn't. I was tired of putting a smile on in public when there were deep and dark feelings inside. I was just tired.

There was a lot of yelling in the bathroom. I yelled over and over words that amounted to, "I'm in control of this situation. You don't have control anymore. I'm in control." The ironic thing was that I was completely out of control.

It was at that time I redirected where the gun was pointed. This time it wasn't to scare her; it was to end the situation. It was to end me. I pointed it at my head first, and then pointed it into my mouth. I remember thinking, *Just squeeze*. The trigger, I remember, seemed to be physically harder and harder to pull; the safety was off, and there was nothing keeping it from going all the way back. I just wanted the trigger to go all the way back.

Then I remember a fleeting thought: *I don't want my children to grow up without a father like I had to. I don't want my mother to be without both of her children.*

I let go of the trigger at that time, and I unloaded the gun and threw it on the bed. "It's over," I said, knowing she was going to call the police. I sat in the living room with the front door wide open so I could be in view of the police when they showed up. I poured a glass of wine and waited.

When they showed up, they took statements and arrested me. Officer Steele from the gas thief incident in the "Sheepdogs" chapter took me to the county jail. That is where I started the longest twenty-seven hours of my life.

That was the day I learned that a person can portray himself to be tough. He can go to the gym five days a week, stand tall, walk proud, and articulate himself in a confident manner, but he cannot hide from—nor can he eternally *resist*—the hurt, anxiety, anger, and isolation he feels because of the events in life he has *overcome* but never *dealt* with. Before he knows it, a small argument lands him with a 9mm handgun in his mouth with no safety and a round in the chamber, and the only thing keeping him from using the muscle on his index finger to squeeze out the hurt, anxiety, depression, and isolation is the thought of his mother, who has already lost one child, and the two kids he doesn't want to grow up like he had to from the age of thirteen—fatherless.

If it weren't for those two fleeting thoughts, I can't say I would have put the gun down that afternoon. I didn't put the gun down because I *wanted* to be alive. I put it down because of reasons outside of my desires. I have always thought suicide is the most cowardly way out and does nothing but show what a selfish attitude a person can have, but it was an option that day. It was a rational option in my mind. Today I'm glad I chose the alternative.

What I will say about that experience goes back to resistance and the idea that man can resist his innermost troubles. He cannot. What he will do, if put in the wrong situation, is find that he has a breaking point. After that day, I have come to the firm belief that everybody has a breaking point. It doesn't matter if life has been a constant struggle or if you have been in a life situation where troubles have been small—breaking points exist for every person alive.

I heard on the news recently about a man in Texas who walked in on a farmhand molesting his four-year-old daughter. The father subsequently beat the pedophile to death on the spot, but he was remorseful and truly apologetic, so the police (at the time of this writing) are not pressing charges. He did what he had to do to protect his daughter, but at the same time he lost all rationality, all temperance, and all composure the second he saw his little girl—a four-year-old princess in his eyes—being brutally attacked by a full-grown man. He broke.

It is the man who allows that point to come when it is avoidable who is weak. It is the man who suppresses emotions and feelings to the point he loses temporary (or permanent) control of his actions, often to his peril and that of others, who is weak. It is the man who is out of control and feeble for allowing those emotions and feelings to control him without asking for help who is weak.

One of the criticisms I had during an annual review at my place of employment was that I didn't ask for help when I may have very well needed it. I remember thinking, *That's the Marine in me. When given a mission, I attempt to complete it at all costs.* I have come to realize that doesn't always work in the civilian world. Unfortunately, it took severe lessons for me to understand.

9.
Friends, Enemies, and the Truth Revealed

It was the weekend after the Thanksgiving Day altercation when I first walked in his office. He had a solid reputation, and he came highly recommended. I expected an older man, taller and with a more traditional haircut that you would expect to be seen on a criminal defense attorney. What greeted me in the front lobby was a man of average height with a head shaved bald and a thick mustache, but Tyson carried himself with the utmost professionalism from the first time I met him, and while he looked like he could have been a biker—albeit in a suit—he was a very proficient attorney.

I remember feeling humiliated that day. There I was, a city councilman for the third largest city in the state of Missouri, and I was consulting with a criminal defense attorney about what would end up being three felony assault counts and a misdemeanor for tampering with evidence. It was the confrontation on Thanksgiving Day that had landed me in the situation. The media had been having a field day with the story since the holiday weekend. An attorney friend of mine advised me to say nothing more than the fact that I was involved in an incident and the investigation was ongoing. The people who were involved in the other party were soaking up their fifteen minutes of fame. It seemed to me that on every news site they could get on, they were claiming I tried to kill them. As earlier stated, the media ran stories for days on end, and one print version ran for over a week; what these media outlets did to continue to make it "news" was put a different twist on each day's story when there was nothing new to report. When I walked into Tyson's office, I was in the middle of the media trial.

While I sat in Tyson's office revisiting the Thanksgiving Day incident, I was distraught. I didn't see that I had done anything wrong and believed it was an act of self-defense. I remember being in disbelief and shock at the severity of the situation. As we came to the conclusion of the discussion, he wanted to talk about the media and how to approach the different outlets. It was the common-sense approach for a public figure who was under investigation, but I was glad we went over the details regardless of that fact. In short, his counsel went something like this: "Say nothing."

After we finished the details on how to handle the different news outlets, he made a comment I will never forget. I had already realized that because I was an elected official, the spotlight would be on me; I had realized in short order the trial-by-media was inevitable. What I didn't realize at the time was the gravity of what he was about to say to me. After the media conversation there was a brief pause. Then, he looked at me with endearment, putting business aside and taking more of a man-to-man approach. He said, "You're about to find out who your true friends and your true enemies are, and have no doubt—by the end of this, you will know exactly who your enemies are."

**

When it came to friends, I found there were very few people I considered friends on a personal level who actually were. Amazingly enough, those in political positions and players in the political party of which I consider myself a part were the least judgmental and most gracious with their sincerity in caring for my situation. Another group of individuals who were most respectful of me, even when they had every opportunity to make a political spectacle, were my city council colleagues. The mayor, Jim O'Neal, and my greatest political opponent on council, Cindy Rushefsky, were examples who represented the rest of the council's actions. The mayor gave me nothing but kind remarks in the media and Councilwoman Rushefsky, after my resignation, wrote an opinion editorial in the newspaper giving me nothing but praise for my leadership. For those actions, and the actions of all of council, I am forever grateful.

I would be remiss if I were to not mention some of the other people who played a major role in my support. My employer at the time was one; in the day and age in which we live, with Missouri being a right to hire/right to fire state, I am appreciative my employer didn't do what, in my mind, would have been understandable. I understand that for a time my name was a liability; him keeping me as an employee is something for which I'm forever grateful. Friends at work, those I met while attending Alcoholics Anonymous, and those who were either gained through council association or on a personal level are ones I will forever have gratitude toward. After finding out how accurate Tyson's words were with regard to enemies, I came to understand and realize how important these relationships were, as they included no judgment, unconditional love, and dedication to the friendship of a person who was publicly scorned for his actions.

I will also never forget the role that my family played in the time that followed. After my eleven-year-old daughter was ridiculed by her gym teacher at school because of me, she still had the capacity of love to tell me, "Daddy, it's okay. Everybody makes mistakes. I still love you, and I will always be your little girl." My son, who had recently approached his teenage years, asked what happened; I told him what I could and was as truthful as I could possibly be given Tyson's request of confidentiality regarding certain facts. My mother and stepfather opened their house to me and allowed me to live there during this time of turmoil; my mother and I have had a tumultuous relationship my entire adult life for many reasons, but her doors were open for me when I needed it most.

I could never forget to mention my guardian angel; I say that with all sincerity. There have been two times in my life when I felt the hand of the Lord on my shoulder; one was in Iraq on May 10, 2005, and the other was during the weeks immediately following my twenty-seven hour stay in Greene County Jail. Jina was one of the first people I talked to after I was released, and her first words were, "Whatever you need, I'm here. However you need me to be there, and whatever you need me to do, I'm here. Don't worry about me or my well-being; you worry about yourself and how I can be there to help." While I had known Jina Lynn for several years in a professional manner, I had come to know her as a personal friend over the few months preceding the New Year. After the New Year, there was never pressure from her—just an endless capacity to love me as a human being and to be there for somebody who was, for the most part, otherwise all alone. Yes, I had friends, but they had their own lives, which I didn't expect them to stop living for me. While I didn't expect this from anybody, she gave it to me.

Those were my friends. Over the next several months, I would come to find how important friendships are and how important it is to appreciate them when they are true and trustworthy. I know it was mentioned in the acknowledgments, but again: To those friends who are reading this book, thank you for what you have given me in your love, dedication, and willingness to allow me to be in your life.

**

For a couple of days after Tyson's comments, I thought about whom I had wronged politically and personally. I wasn't somebody you were going to search the web to find dirt on. Am I a perfect man? Not by any stretch of the imagination, but I didn't have love-children, wasn't in any sort of abnormal debt, and had made no unscrupulous pacts for political gain. The people I had most wronged in my life were people in my family as a result of extremely poor decision-making skills, my underlying emotional and psychological troubles, and my use of alcohol as a medication over the years, especially after Iraq. As unfortunate as it is, I came to realize that if the fact was that I had enemies, they were going to be people I thought to be friends and socialized with to that point. They were going to be people who looked me straight-faced with a smile and told me they were my friends.

This type of betrayal would not have been new to me, though. I remember the first taste I had of this; it was during my tenure on the council. I don't remember the particular issue, but I had taken a minority stand and it was written about in the newspaper. At the time, the prominent newspaper, the *Springfield News-Leader,* offered the ability for readers to post comments about any story they wanted to online. Unfortunately, as stated in another chapter, they could do so under any user name of their choice and didn't have to be held accountable for their statements. (Not to get off track, but it was quite interesting to see the commenters' change of tune once the paper changed the comments section format and forced the use of names via Facebook.)

With this particular news story, there was a comment that said (to paraphrase), "I think Nick Ibarra just needs to shut his mouth, take care of his family, and go make some rubber hoses." Now, one may ask, "What in the world does that mean?" Exactly! For somebody to make that comment, in particular the part about the rubber hose, he would have to know me personally and know exactly what I did at that time for a vocation. While the company I worked for did make rubber hoses, the company's web site discussed dozens of other products it made and listed the fifteen-plus stores it had in the country. To know that one of our branch's particular products was rubber hoses was to know me personally. The person who posted that comment was somebody who knew me well enough to know exactly the product I sold; therefore, in my mind, he was somebody who was willing to look me straight-faced and with a smile and nod and then turn around and anonymously post a personal attack because he disagreed with my politics.

Back to the situation.

So, there I was. For the first time, I was in a position where I would "find out who my enemies were." It didn't take a week before I would realize how true his statement was. The first tip I got was from a source who crossed my path and asked if I knew about the letter that had gone around. I didn't know and stated so. It was explained to me that there was a secret mail delivery to every house in my neighborhood about the Thanksgiving Day incident. The person or persons who made this delivery cooked up a typed letter that gave police report numbers for two different incidents in which I had previously been involved. The media was contacted by one of the residents who received the letter and the news coverage started.

The issue is not the fact that the media found out. At this point in the game, I didn't expect them not to—quite frankly, I felt a sense of relief that they had. They could get it over and done with, because I knew it was coming. The issue in my mind was how the letter creation and delivery was done and the fact that the person who appeared to be behind it was somebody I'd called a friend for several years, but that same person would straight-faced lie to me about it, which I believe to be the case. The interesting part is that the person I believe did this has a decent amount of intelligence, but didn't have the common sense to think that all evidence would point straight to that person. I say this because the police report numbers listed are ones only this person would have known to look for due to the nature of the reports.

In the end, this was the first of two instances in which people I trusted with my children—and whose children played with mine—with whom I ate dinner, spent holidays, and had what I thought were close ties completely disregarded our friendship for no other reason than spite, the cause of which I'm unsure of. While this was an action that definitely changed that particular friendship, the worst was yet to come when finding out who my enemies really were.

**

I remember the first time I met the man we will call Jess. He approached me as I was unpacking my personal goods into the first house I ever bought. It was a small three-bedroom home on the west side of town in a quiet neighborhood that people didn't go to unless they had business there.

"You were in the Marines," he asked. I told him I was; I knew he asked because of the bumper sticker I had on the back of my Jeep Cherokee. He said he had also been in the Marines, so there was an immediate connection. It came to pass that our children were in the same age group and ended up being neighborhood chums for the next six years. As the years passed, Jess and I became close friends. At times we were inseparable. There were periods of time when we would meet up Friday after work to spend weekends together, and the only time we were apart until the following Sunday evening would be to sleep. Our kids would be together all weekend, and it was almost like two families joined as one for a weekend here and there.

When I ran for city council and while I was on city council, he would help me with my speeches; he was a communications professional with good knowledge on the topic. When my kids' dog passed away, it was Jess who helped me bury the canine. When he and his wife separated—around the same time my ex-wife and I did—we leaned on each other for comfort. The list of things we did together could go on, but the point I believe to be clear: The relationship I had with Jess wasn't one that meant little to me. It wasn't long after the Thanksgiving Day incident that I would find out just what I meant to him.

**

The first time I remember seeing Jess for who he truly was, without the blinders of the friendship, was after one of my first court appearances for the Thanksgiving Day incident. I was on the phone with Tyson and going over the morning's events, and he mentioned to me he had received some of the preliminary reports from the county prosecutor.

We were talking about the strengths and the weaknesses of our case. At one point in the conversation, he said, "Something that is not going to help is the statement your friend Jess gave to the highway patrol." After inquiring what Tyson meant by that comment, it became clear that Jess had stated to the highway patrol that what happened was intentional on my part, that I had intentionally dragged one of the two men in my car.

In writing this book, I have made a habit of being careful when it comes to making outright accusations as compared to saying I believe something to be true. I will continue to be cautious, but there is not an ounce of doubt in my firm belief that he lied and did so knowingly.

While I was physically ill after hearing this, I was even more ill after reading the full report at a later time. The statement he made to the highway patrol was such an exaggeration that if he hadn't penetrated my trust in him so badly, I would have chalked it up to him maybe misunderstanding what it was I told him or maybe even a lapse of clarity due to the time that had passed since the incident.

While I could have almost bought into a misunderstanding if he would have told me so, he hasn't called me since his statements to the police were made public.

It was this particular experience that brought me to the understanding that true friends are hard to come by. You really experience betrayal when you have a "friend" you will break bread with, share parts of your life with, and discuss your innermost thoughts with who, in the end, had malicious intentions. All he was looking for was the opportunity to take action.

I will sum this story up by recalling the movie *The General's Daughter*. This was a John Travolta movie in which he was a military investigator. The plot surrounded the murder of a young female officer that took place on a military base. The victim, who lived on the base, happened to be the daughter of a general. At one point in the movie, the general and Travolta were discussing the case and the general asked what could be worse than murder in response to a comment Travolta made about something being worse than being murdered. At the end of the movie, it came to pass that the general knew of the details surrounding his daughter's murder and was willing to cover them up for the sake of the base and his honor. One of the last lines of the movie was Travolta basically saying, "You once asked what could be worse than murder. The answer is betrayal."

I have been hurt in my life many times by friends, family, and all types of people with whom I've had relationships. I have been lied to many times, as well. One thing that I have only felt once, and don't ever care to feel again, is the sense of betrayal I felt when I found out what Jess had done.

**

I have come a long way from the man I was before January 1, 2012, and I have been at more and more ease with the events that took place. In the immediate aftermath of Thanksgiving Day and New Year's, I was very resentful and carried a lot of hatred toward not only those who did what they did, but also toward me, for putting myself in a position to disgrace the name that my father gave me. Knowing that, forgiveness is something that I understand will need to be a part of my heart's desire in order to get past what has happened.

My relationship with the Lord has grown day by day, and I am almost to a point that I resent not being able to forgive both myself and the one person who will take the longest to forgive—Jess. In my heart and in my mind, I know what the right thing to do is. I have made it a small goal to forgive those who have trespassed against me as I would want those I have wronged to forgive me. I'm not there yet, but the train is still moving.

10.

The Sentence

In the fall of 2013, after two years of legal issues hanging over my head, I pleaded guilty to the crimes I was charged with: Two counts of felony assault and one count of tampering with evidence, both for the 2011 Thanksgiving Day incident involving me following the reckless driver into a really bad situation; and one count of unlawful use of a weapon for the situation that occurred on New Year's Day of 2012 involving my ex-wife that started as a disagreement and quickly spun completely out of control. I pleaded guilty to four felonies.

In the two years since the incidents, the same two years I have been writing what you have read to this point, I went through much counseling to deal with depression and PTSD. I have had two years of sobriety and two years of finding a new me. I have done my very best to improve my relationship with my two children. Through the darkest hours of my life, Jina stood by my side. Through these two years, the most difficult time of my life, I gained a better relationship with my Heavenly Father than I have ever had. For those things, I'm grateful I had the two years. However much there was to endure, I have grown in strength emotionally and physically, and that is something I wouldn't trade if I could.

Then came January 9, 2014. That morning, I faced the judge who was to sentence me for the crimes to which I pleaded guilty. My attorney and I decided to reject the plea bargain offered by the prosecuting attorney and instead put my future at the mercy and in the hands of the judge presiding over my charges.

One of the more difficult issues I knew I would have to face was the response of the public due to the picture painted by much of the media. Regardless of how the law is rendered and the justice system operates, the media's job is to secure good ratings. Exacerbated headlines do just that. So, regardless of how my sentencing went, unless I received the maximum sentence of twenty-two years in prison, which the media portrayed as inevitable, there would be people who were going to accuse me of being let off easy.

On the morning I was to be sentenced, I woke and went to the gym to walk on the treadmill and studied the statement I was to make to the judge. Afterward, I dressed in my suit and went to wake Jina. Leaning over her and offering her a kiss, I woke her and my heart grew heavy knowing this would quite possibly be the last time I would be able to wake her in such a manner before being incarcerated.

She woke and made me a cup of hot chocolate, and we talked for a while. I then made my way to the courthouse. When I walked into the courtroom, it was with the support of about fifteen people I call family and the closest of friends, all of whom I'm forever grateful to have.

The judge called the court to order. He heard the arguments of both the prosecution and the defense. Both were well grounded, and in the end, both sides were given some of what they asked and denied other things they asked; my immediate future was a true compromise. The prosecution wanted me to be incarcerated for 120 days, have at least 1 of the felonies remain on my record permanently, and remain on probation for 5 years after being released from incarceration. We asked for strict probation that upon completion would allow my criminal record to be expunged. We also asked that I not be made to serve time incarcerated, given my progress made in counseling, self, and sobriety, and also due to my responsibilities as a father and employee.

After the arguments were given, the judge made his decision: Five years' probation, upon which successfully completed, my criminal record would be erased, but not before serving one hundred twenty days of incarceration. After the sentence was given, I was told I was allowed some very quick goodbyes.

I turned from the judge to my supporters who attended court with me. I first saw my son, who had tears rolling from his eyes; then my focus turned to my daughter, the view the same. I hugged them tight and told them how dearly I loved them.

The only other thing I remember before being led away was holding Jina's face in my handcuffed hands, kissing her lips, and sharing the panic with her in the decision that was rendered by the judge. I was then led away by the bailiff.

**

The first three weeks of my incarceration was far different from the rest. Because of my position in local politics, there was heavy media attention given to my situation. Because of that, I was placed in confined protective custody. For twenty-two to twenty-three hours per day, I was in a cell by myself with little to no human contact. For one or two hours per day I was allowed out of my cell to shower, make phone calls, and have a little time to walk around. When in my cell, I spent my time reading (mostly scripture), writing letters, sleeping, and doing what exercise I could.

It was after about two weeks that the psychological effects of being confined to a cell, alone in my thoughts and with the minimal human interaction the experience possessed, began to fray my nerves. At times it was overwhelming, and toward the end of the experience I fully believed I was on the verge of, if not in the beginning stages of, a psychological and nervous breakdown.

I have been told since that some would love that time and experience away from the hustle and bustle of life. I have no problem saying to those people that until they lock themselves in a bathroom with only a pen, paper, random books of no interest, a Bible, and a mattress with a blanket for an extended period of time, they cannot begin to understand how ignorant they sound. I will profess that what did keep me sane were calls home, scriptural study, and prayers.

After twenty-one and a half days in isolation, I was allowed to move to an area populated with inmates who had medical conditions, both physical and psychological, keeping me semi-segregated. For the next three months and one week, I was in a population that would allow me to come to understand the criminal mindset in a way few do. I was also allowed to see the fact that each individual has a unique story. Whether they were incarcerated for domestic assault, bank robbery, offenses against children, or murder, inmates of the penal system are all human beings with personalities, stories, and lives that have been forever altered. As difficult as it was to accept and embrace, Jina wrote something that forever changed my view: "Keep in mind the men you are in there with are lost sheep of the Lord's fold; have compassion and know the Atonement of Christ is equally available to them as it is to you and me."

During the course of the 120 days, I was able to make strides in spiritual growth and reflect on life and how it was versus how I wanted it to be. It was a pause in life for me to grab my footing and create a blueprint of how I wanted to move forward in life. As difficult as the time was, it did serve a greater purpose that was for the betterment of my mind and soul.

Time and again I appealed to the judge's compassion and requested early release, which is a standard request. After it became clear that the judge was not going to allow my request, I was let down in hope but not surprised, but then came Brian, one of my two last cell mates. A former military pilot, he'd led a long life with much struggle. One night he asked me about my faith, and that night turned into several days of interrogation about what I believed as a Christian. By the time I left, he was determined to be released and find members of my church to teach him more and move forward with what he believed to be "the truth." We agreed in the end that we were put in a cell together for a reason. If, in fact, he changes his life for the better, I will be proud of him and happy for him, but knowing that I was given the opportunity to share with him how to make that change made the 120 days well worth every second.

Overall, during the experience of being incarcerated for the short amount of time that I was, I bore heavy burdens—some of the heaviest I have ever experienced: Guilt, remorse, and sorrow. At the same time, I had some of the longest and most sincere laughs I have ever experienced in life. Most of them came with two of my cell mates, Danny and Mark. Lest I forget to mention, I was given the opportunity to try "prison pizza," which is a casserole of Ramen noodles, hot corn chips, jalapeño cheese, and diced summer sausage all mushed together and made into the shape of a pizza...Don't knock it 'til you try it!

As my incarceration came to a close, I viewed it as possibly the most difficult experience in my life, and then the end of a chapter. Another defining moment ended.

It was time for me to look forward, to learn from the past but refuse to let it hinder me. It was time to grab Jina and the kids, follow the path my Heavenly Father would lay before me, and move beyond the fray.

11.
Beyond the Fray

When I first began writing *Beyond the Fray*, there was no intention of doing anything but fulfilling a request my counselor and my future wife (Jina) made: To write down and keep a regular journal of my thoughts, feelings, and perspective on life during the months after the life-altering events that occurred on Thanksgiving Day of 2011 and New Year's Day of 2012.

What it has become, over time, is a story I wanted to share with others. The reason I want to share it isn't to brag about my experiences, to justify anything I have done, or to simply tell a story. The reason is to share this particular chapter of *Beyond the Fray* and help you understand that what I have learned and hope to pass on was not primarily learned in a classroom; it was learned through life's experiences. Through these very personal experiences and working to deal with them, I have come to realize that the hurt, anger, sadness, and anxiety—the "fray" in life—doesn't have to be there. I have learned that there is an easier, simpler way to approach life. There doesn't have to be darkness.

I was released from jail after New Year's Day of 2012. As stated in previous chapters, at that time I knew something in life had to change. I immediately began to receive counseling with the help of the Veteran's Administration, and I began taking my relationship with God more seriously than ever before. I began to explore what a world without hurt, depression, anxiety, and pain looked like. Through it all, and over the course of the three-year paradigm shift I made in life, things have happened that led me to believe that I have done a fair job in my work toward becoming a better individual. I have been honored with a leadership position in my church. With the encouragement of the VA, I have become certified as Peer Specialist in Missouri to help others who have had similar experiences to mine. Most of all, I have actually been able to help others, even if only in part, see a bigger picture and how they can find a better course in particular situations and in life as a whole.

In short, what I found was and is magnificent; if for no other reason, I wanted to turn my "journal" into book format to share what I had been through and what I found and how it has fundamentally changed my view on life, relationships, and the blessings we have been given in our existence and our journeys in life.

As we move forward, I want to ensure you that what I share is as much for me as it is for you. It is not my desire to seem like I'm doing anything more than sharing what I have learned and reminding myself of those same principles and values. In that, I sincerely intend the use of words such as *I, me, we,* and *you* to all be interchangeable.

As we go through each of the ten principles, a clear fact we need to understand is that finding our "best selves" is not a cookie-cutter process. Each of our experiences has led us to a place that is our own, and each of us will have to take our own paths to happiness. What I have found works for me has been adapted from others. These principles have also been found by making my own path with the knowledge I have gained through counseling, study, instruction, and even the certification courses I was asked to take so I could help others!

I hope that in whatever form these ideas take, you are able to use them if you are a person seeking a different way of life. If you are a person who has a friend or family member in need, I hope that the previous chapters have served to give insight to certain things in your loved one's life and their perception of it. Further, I hope this book as a whole will in some way help you help that loved one, even if it is simply being a more understanding family member or friend.

That being said, let's explore a path we may want to travel—a path that takes us beyond the fray.

* *

Are you willing to fight to get your life back? In all honesty, this question has to be answered with a resounding *yes* in order for anything else to work. In order to have a life of general happiness and the least amount of regrets, you have to want it. It's not about what *I* want; it's not about what your family and friends are saying you *should* do; it's not about what you think is right. It's about truly having a passion to wake up without worry, without fear, and without any hesitation of facing life on life's terms.

The truth of the matter is that when I finally came to the place in life where I *knew* something had to change, I was in a situation in which any other alternative would have led to a path of destruction, commonly referred to as "rock bottom." While I hope that is not where you are, I equally hope you don't have to get there to make the decision. (If you are there, the good news is that the only way left to go is up!) Given that you very well may not be at rock bottom, you absolutely have the option to fight or not.

We have that option every day. We can decide to embrace every negative thought that comes our way. We can decide to embrace bad memories that keep our hearts in dark places. We can decide to be upset about the driver in front of us who just cut us off and is now going five miles below the speed limit. If we want change, though, we have to embrace the fact that those things are not taking us anywhere positive—whether it's depression, loneliness, anxiety, PTSD, or out-of-control anger that plagues us. If we keep doing what we've always done, we'll always get what we've always gotten. What we will have to do to find a better life is always focus on our every action. New actions we aren't accustomed to will quite often have to be forced before they come naturally.

It's not easy. It hurts. Sometimes I hurt so bad that I have cried; sometimes all I could do is sit in wonder at how things in my life had turned out. Sometimes I was mad at others and at myself, and sometimes I was mad at God.

What I learned when I started dealing with those emotions is that I had suppressed so much for so long that I didn't even realize what I was doing. However, when I found that closet and allowed it to be open, I was able to fight the demons of my past and the skeletons inside. When I opened that closet, I was faced with an option: Am I going to face this fight head on and make it the primary focus of my life, or am I going to go through the motions until it gets too hard and then quit?

When I got to a place in which the answer was the former, I was ready. Again, you have to decide to do it for yourself, not for anybody or anything else. In the end, it is you who has to live with yourself; I have to do the same. Relationships come and go, as do jobs and every other event in life. Deciding to fight to get your life back for anything or anybody but yourself is setting yourself up for failure before you even begin.

If you are that person who wants a spiritual serenity, an emotional happiness, and a life free from self-created turmoil, both emotional and physical, read on.

**

Your change must be your physical priority. It's really that simple. Above all else in the physical world, you becoming a better you must be the priority.

I remember when I was told this the first time. Basically, during the journey of becoming a better me, I had to face the fact that I would have to change where I was spending social time, who I was spending it with, and what I was doing—in part because of my alcohol use, but also in part because of the person it made me. You can't spend all your spare time with people who are constantly upset and have negative attitudes and then expect to be any different.

For those of us who deal with medical issues that require the attention of professionals, we have to accept the fact that we are going to face the stigma of being "different." I have found three types of people when dealing with people who recognize people with medical issues: The people who use the issues against us, the people who coddle us because they see us as frail, and the people who accept us and treat us with compassion but at the same time are able to be "real" with us.

We have to decide how much of the first two we can take, and then we have to decide how to navigate our behaviors and decisions in situations with each type of person. "John always makes comments about my bipolar disorder that make me feel inferior," for instance. When we face a similar situation, we have to ask two questions. The first is about interpretation. Are we correctly interpreting what he is saying, or are we being hypersensitive because of our own insecurities? The second is asked if we are correct in our interpretation—how do we address his comments? While the simple answer may be to approach him and tell him our feelings, we have to accept that he may continue to make the comments. The question then becomes whether or not our becoming a better person is the priority. If it is, are we willing to do whatever we have to in order to become that better person?

Am I saying you have to be willing to leave your spouse, end friendships, or abandon family relationships in pursuit of that goal? No. That is not for me to say, and it is not a decision for anybody but you to make. What I am saying is that none of us deserves to be demeaned and sometimes even emotionally abused because our struggles are different than those of others. If we are not respected, if we do not feel loved, if we do not feel cherished and worthwhile for who are in any particular relationship, the question arises as to whether that is the type of relationship we want or need. Is it the type of relationship that is going to help us find the best life we can, to find happiness where we used to only be sad, to find light where there used to only be dark?

The same concept goes for the coddling friend or family member. "Don't bring this up to Susan, it will only reignite old memories, and we have to protect her," for instance. That is something we also need to question in the same manner as the hurtful comments. Is it helpful or hurtful? If it is hurtful, how do we address it? If my concerns and requests are not well received, how far am I willing to take my concerns in order to ensure my happiness? Is my happiness the priority, or am I willing to accept discontent in order to keep a particular relationship?

Along with personal relationships, social interactions that take place in our spare time, where we work, where we go to church, and during every other activity we participate in should be evaluated with integrity and sincerity. Through the same principled questions as above, we need to create clear boundaries about what is acceptable and what promotes a spiritual, emotional, and physical ascendancy to happiness.

When we do find those relationships, activities, and social interactions that are meaningful, bring joy, and are enjoyed with a sincere companion (that of a friend or family member or are romantic), we must also do the hard work of accepting it, embracing it, and letting that relationship make us better.

Many of us have always been "bad pickers." We choose friends and significant others and keep in close contact with family that keep us down. You know what I mean—the conversations that are full of gossip or can't stay in a positive tone. It's almost like a magnet, and when we find good, wholesome, and healthy relationships that only speak and do good, we flip that magnet over and push those people away.

Stop doing it. Let the good in…And to be clear, you don't have to call all your friends that typically have a negative aura and tell them how bad they are and that they don't have a place in your life. Simply excuse yourself in a respectful manner whenever negative situations arise. I promise, they'll catch on to what's happening.

What it comes down to is this: In order to find the peace and serenity that I believe everybody desires and deserves, we have to be willing to place our own lives as the priority as we journey through them. It is difficult to be the best spouse, parent, brother, sister, son, daughter, friend, or employee when you can't be the best you that you can offer yourself. In order to do that, finding the best you must supersede everything else in the physical world.

**

The value and reward of a personal relationship with God is without measure. Quite frankly, if it weren't for the progress and improvement I have had in my relationship with God, I wouldn't be half as successful as I believe I have been in my progress as an individual. There are several actions we can take, namely prayer (1 Thes. 5:16), scriptural study (Josh 1:8), attending church (1 John 1:3), and, yes, tithing (Mal. 3:10)), in our daily lives to improve that relationship. Like any other relationship, it takes both parties' involvement in order for the relationship to bear the most fruit possible.

In short order, we can find through the above-mentioned actions the ability to participate in a relationship in which success is solely dependent on us. In the physical world, the interactions we have with our fellow man are going to involve many unknown factors. In a relationship with God, we know what he expects; what was expected in the beginning has always been expected, is expected now, and will always be expected.

By keeping up our end of the bargain and following through with his wishes for us, there is an abundance of blessings we can receive—namely the emotional and spiritual gratification of having a relationship with the planter of trees and hanger of planets, and that we know him and he knows us. Through scripture study, we learn many lessons that can guide us through life. We learn that while Job was tested time and again, he remained faithful and was rewarded in the end. We learn the value of being pure in heart, making only peace, and seeking only righteous things will allow us to naturally become stronger people, happier people, and better people (Matt. 5). (When you have the time and the earnest and open heart to ponder it, read and then read again and ponder Matthew 5:1–15; imagine how transformational it would be if we all decided to live by those verses!)

Here's the catch with your personal relationship with God: It's yours and nobody else's, but with that comes something for sincere consideration—other people who have a relationship with God have that same ownership. While there are several discussions in the Bible about reproof or correction, I have come to the firm belief that accusations, humiliation, and scorn are not Christlike. We should not accept it of ourselves or others. The question of the beam and mote and the call to cast the first stone should be considerations we live by when evaluating what to say and to whom (Matt. 7:3-5; John 8:1-11). Likewise, we cannot control how others perceive what a relationship with God looks like. We have to be levelheaded and evaluate situations of confrontation and controversy, being sure to remember that there is a time and place to discuss our shortfalls and the shortfalls of others—when invited. We always need to be as respectful and diligent as possible when dealing with those we love enough to share that intimate part of life with, regardless of how we are treated in return (Matt. 7:12).

The relationship we have with God is one that will guide us in difficult times, one we can rejoice in during times of triumph, and one that can only make us better human beings as we attempt to follow in the steps of Jesus the Christ by way of a truly humble and meek heart.

* *

Be objective and take a really good look in the mirror. When analyzing our own beings and who we are, one of the easiest things to do is to look at opportunities and strengths—things that are good about us, our attributes. Attributes are always good to consider and remember as an encouragement about who we can continue to be with regard to those particular strengths and what we *can* do. It's another thing to truly look at our character defects, faults, and flaws. Who wants to do that?! The truth is that the biggest part of your willingness to fight to take your life back is going to be the battle you have within yourself.

When I earlier discussed hitting rock bottom, there was a reason. For many others who have traveled a path similar to mine, it took hitting rock bottom (as I did) for them to start a new and better way. Whether rock bottom is divorce, death, or sitting in a jail cell, it took a moment in life that was so profoundly negative for us to realize that, "Okay, this is bad, and maybe I am the cause of it." Whether it was alcohol, anger, depression, or some other cause, our arrogance often had us so blinded by what we were doing and to whom that the idea we were causing our own destruction was impossible for us to see. Clearly, it was the ubiquitous other person's fault. "If they would only do this or that, be better at one thing or another, or just listen to me and do what I say, none of the negative things in my life would be happening, and we could all just live in peace," we proclaim.

To say the following is quite difficult: "Dear Self: You are horrible at relationships not because you don't have the ability to do better, but because you are too blind to even notice that you are bad at them. While we're at it, Self, your anger is out of control. Do you realize you yelled at your two-year-old son because the dishes weren't done last night? Oh, by the way, did you see how guilty you made your wife feel for not wanting to be intimate with you after she worked twelve hours? Man, what's your problem?!"

The good news is that this part is only the beginning. Immediately following the not-so-fun step of counting our faults in detail, we must begin the work of doing something about them. As with all the things we will discuss in this chapter, and things not mentioned but that come to your mind for later study, there is a plethora of information available in libraries and through professionals, self-help groups, and reliable sources on the Internet that can only deepen your knowledge of how to take the steps necessary to becoming a better and more fulfilled person. Let this chapter be the beginning and *only* the beginning.

One thing that often helps us find those issues we wish to face is the help of a loved one who is sincere and is not going to turn your humble request into a discussion of all the wrongs you have done without showing any compassion or humility. Another thing that often helps through this process is to find an outside third party that can assist. In Alcoholics Anonymous and other like-minded organizations, they are called sponsors.

Taking an honest inventory of who we are, faults and all, is extremely difficult, but absolutely necessary. Help—sincere help—is a great blessing that should be used if at all possible.

* *

In all things from this moment forward, be meek and humble. Two of the most valuable tools many of us have had during our struggles with the problems we have faced in life have been perimeters and barriers. Perimeters are lines we don't let others cross; barriers are the ways in which we keep breaches in our perimeters from happening. In our lives and our relationships, these tools help us keep who we are inside and what we feel to ourselves.

One type of barrier can take the form of us setting up walls that keep people out of any discussion regarding our emotional life. Another can take the form of refusing to admit when we are wrong or have done something unkindly; it can also take the form of a general sense of confrontation, arrogance, and sometimes even having hostility toward the ones we love and care for—much less strangers and acquaintances. Many of us also—and I am a walking example— "shut down" whenever we feel our emotional security is threatened. We intentionally shut off all emotion to stay safe in a hostile situation.

I have found that these walls are ones that are erected for protection. If we perceive a loved one is mad at us, we decide to take an "I don't care about them, anyway" approach. If we *think* someone is going to accuse us of something, we set up our defensive postures without first inspecting the situation. It will typically follow that we become the proactive aggressors so that we don't have to be attacked first. If we perceive a significant other is going to hurt us, we withdraw emotionally and sometimes run before we are run from. When we believe we are going to be hurt in any way, we set up walls protecting us from the threats over which we have little, if any, control.

The second problem we run into is pride. As we have struggled through the situations in life that made us who we are, we have often fallen prey to the idea that since we have survived war, abuse, addiction, and so on, we know everything there is to know about those topics and more. We cannot be told anything new; there is no insight to life we haven't already considered. This can take the form of anything, from the actual experiences we have had to mundane topics such as current events in the news. We can't be told that our point of view or the knowledge we have is wrong. If it was, that would mean we were wrong, and if we were wrong, then we would be less than what we hoped to be.

Here's some news about barriers and pride: With barriers and pride, we make little, if any, progress. When we shut down, we keep out the experience of emotion and its ability to amplify the beauty of the human experience. Even more, when we keep barriers and pride in our personality, we are going to consistently keep ourselves from creating healthy relationships with those we love and with new people who will inevitably come into our lives.

What does it mean to be meek and humble? Adequate consideration has to be given to these concepts, for the fact is that if we haven't practiced them, we may not know them. If we don't know them, we need to learn them. We need to learn about being meek and humble not only in the traditional sense, but we also need to change our behaviors so that being meek and humble becomes second nature.

Ulisses Soares gracefully explained that "being meek does not mean weakness, but it does mean behaving with goodness and kindness, showing strength, serenity, healthy self-worth, and self-control." We can combine C.S. Lewis's belief that "humility is not thinking less of yourself; rather, thinking of yourself less," and Ralph Waldo Emerson's profound concept that "a great man is always willing to be little" in order to learn about humility. Making those two ideas the centerpieces of our behavior would make a profound shift in the tone of many of our personalities.

Imagine what would happen if when we were upset, we could calm ourselves with self-control that is optimistic rather than the lack of self-control that shuts all emotion down. What if when we are being told we are wrong, we lower our pride just enough to say, "I'm going to listen to what I'm being told because what I thought I knew *could* be wrong?" What if when we are confronted with adversity, scorn, or even confrontation, we simply use kindness and serenity in our tone as we respond with confidence, ensuring we have done everything possible to show peace and strength in conjunction with one another?

One guiding principle I have used in many situations—actually, as many situations as possible, good and bad—is that Jesus should not only be my savior, but also my role model. When we are confronted in public, remember how much self-control Jesus had when he responded to the Pharisees asking the question about whether the adultress should be stoned: "Let him who is without sin cast the first stone," (John 8). He did not hatefully rebuke; he did not raise his voice; he also did not cower, hide, or withdraw in the face of confrontation. Instead, he was meek and humble, but strong and firm. What a phenomenal example to strive for!

It takes practice. There will be mistakes, and there will be backslides. Those things are all okay. What is most important is for us to remember is that we got to where we are traveling our own paths; similarly, we will have to find our own paths to the better life, and those paths should be with strides toward daily progress. As the Alcoholics Anonymous saying goes, "We seek progress, not perfection."

**

You can only control yourself and your actions, and that's where the buck stops. That's right. You are in control of you and only you. If somebody cuts you off in traffic, you can only control how *you* react. If a loved one treats you unkindly, you can't change them, but you can change how you react to them. The possibilities and examples are eternal, but what's not eternal is what you can control. We only have control over ourselves, and little more.

As I discuss this particular topic, think back to the discussion we recently had of relationships and how we react to how loved ones treat us. Remember the emphasis placed on explaining concerns to others but not trying to control their actions or reactions. The discussion was based on the concept of controlling our actions, but also having healthy boundaries with those we love in regard to their treatment of us. Along the same line of thought, let's look a little more inward.

Soon after the situation which I was jailed for on New Year's Day, I was having a difficult time with my relationship with my children. Distraught, I would worry myself about the father I *had* been. Both my children had seen me intoxicated. The same two children had been at the brunt of my anger even when they didn't cause it. They had absolutely seen me at my worst.

When I began to work on me, I wanted so badly to make up for the person I had been to them, but I couldn't. I just couldn't. I had to accept what had happened and what I had done. I had to accept that from their births to their pre-teen years, my life had been a disaster and I had taken them along on that journey.

I was told that as long as I held onto wanting to fix or undo what happened, I was not going to progress. What I had was a road ahead of me. While on that road, I had to let go of my past mistakes. I should never forget; I should make amends when and where possible, but I should understand there was no undoing things that had been done.

I wanted to share as much time with them as possible to somehow get back the time I had lost, but they are teenagers now. They have many other priorities that come before sitting at Dad's house and spending time with him. It tore me up at first, and I wanted to dwell on that.

I soon realized that this was my first big test. Was I going to let go of my past and make the best of my future on the terms life was giving me? If so, I had to realize that the children were going to make the decisions they were going to make, and there was nothing I could do about it. Like any other relationship, this would be one that took both parties to participate in.

Sure, I could guilt them into coming over and visiting. I could go to court and tell a judge that the parenting plan in my divorce decree wasn't being followed. I could do many things to invade their space and their decisions. They were teenagers, though, and to take that experience from them to try and make up for my personal shortcomings and guilt would have been nothing short of trying to control their actions for my personal, selfish gain.

The same could be said for a husband, wife, brother, sister, or any loved one who lives by a premise that their wants or needs are more important than those of the person with whom they are interacting. To try and control another person for selfish purposes is not only disrespectful; it is unhealthy for all involved.

This concept is similar to the "live and let live" concept, but with a little more intellect than a bumper sticker slogan. There is no serenity in worrying ourselves sick about what others may or may not do, think, or like. They are their own people, and we are our own people.

When we start to worry about the control in our own lives and stop worrying so much about how to control others, there is a sense of calm and peace that will invade our very being. Additionally, it is an awesome experience when you come to the place that says, "I have control of my life, my actions, my decisions, my emotions, and that is all I need. This is good." There is power in letting go, and when we can do it with integrity, we will find a joy that has never been felt. I have felt it. I dare you to try.

* *

Network with those who can help you on your journey. Whatever it is we experience in life—emotional scars, medically diagnosed psychological struggles, or anything else—we are not experiencing it alone. There are many people who have been where we are right now. Some of them were in this darkness or struggle two years ago; others were here twenty years ago. Those who have been here and have found a way out have so much knowledge to share, as do medical professionals. Many books have been written and research done on our exact struggles!

That's the good news. The next bit of good news is that they are everywhere and willing to help. As hard as it may be, especially in the beginning, to seek help, what we gain from sharing our lives, our struggles, our fears and pains with others is that it works itself out for the better over the course of time. Through others' experiences and advice, we are able to try new things, practice new behaviors, and find new lenses through which we view our lives, our past, and the possibilities of our futures.

Another thing I have also found extremely therapeutic is what actually happens *as* we talk to those who are there to help. First, often times, as we begin to explain our feelings and thoughts, we find that just saying them out loud allows us to hear truth and reality, but it also allows us to hear the sometimes irrational or illogical things that go through our minds. Further, as we talk about the issues over and over, we are able to view them as a story in our own history—something that has made our past, but doesn't have to form our future. Eventually, we learn not how to forget it, but how to accept the past for what it is and grasp the truth that the past doesn't *have* to define who we become.

If we sometimes don't see the reality and truth, the irrationality or illogical nature of our thoughts and feelings, be sure that the helpful third party we are talking to will. As individuals who have the expertise, whether through education or experience, they can walk us through the problems, concerns, and memories that plague our innermost selves. Further, they can help us find the answers that will allow us to address our experiences with positivity and optimism, which is true progress. That is the progress we must seek in order to have better lives for ourselves and the friends and family who surround us.

**

Accepting our past for what it is, but refusing to let it enable self-destruction. While there are many of us who fall into depression, anxiety, and other emotional or psychological struggles through natural chemistry, most of us have also experienced abuse, neglect, sexual assault, war, and many other events that were extremely traumatic. Some of these traumatic experiences last only ten seconds, such as a car accident that caused a loved one's death. Some may have lasted a year or two, such as war. Unfortunately, some may have lasted eighteen years or more, in the instance of child neglect or abuse that was physical, sexual, or both.

All of these experiences are ours. We own them. They are in our heads. They have plagued us, and we experience post-traumatic stress, depression, feelings of guilt, paranoia, anxiety, remorse, hyper-vigilance, anger, and many, many other emotions that negatively impact us on a daily basis. Many times we don't realize how the feelings and struggles we face are rooted in and are partially, if not fully, a result of those past life experiences. In the end, the conflict these emotions cause in our daily lives creates a self-destructive path we don't even see happening.

We should never be asked to forget or pretend our experiences never happened. However, in order to get past them, we must address them and deal with them and how they affect us. As we do that very difficult thing, we will find progress happening naturally.

When I first walked into the VA for counseling, I wasn't even sure I had a problem. Further, being a tough Marine, I was sure that if I *did* have PTSD, some counseling—simply talking about my feelings—was not going to just fix the problem.

What I learned first was that the "problem" is not going to be "fixed." What could happen, though, was that I could learn how being irate that the dishes weren't done last night was tied to me not having control. If I could tie those two things together, I could tie another knot in that same string that explained how the fact that I desired complete control had to do with me being on forty-seven missions in Iraq—a place I didn't always have control. At that time, that lack of control could mean that I would have no warning a roadside bomb was about to detonate within feet of my Humvee. I must now ask how logical it is to say that if the dishes aren't done, a roadside bomb could go off and we could all die. It's illogical, maybe, but for years it caused anxiety and anger that wasn't necessary. Subconsciously, I was very angry about all of this, and it was causing me to suffer in much of my life experiences.

As we address the skeletons in our closets and the ghosts in our pasts, we are able to recognize how they affect us and our daily behaviors. As we are able to assess how our behaviors are related to our pasts, we are able to see the red flags that spark those sometimes subconscious reactions to events in life that we don't control. Further, we become able to recognize those adverse reactions and behaviors in real time. As we do that, we are able to practice the meek and humble attitudes we seek in real time, as the difficult situations in life occur.

**

Forgive always, even when forgiveness isn't sought. For many of us, forgiveness has been one of the hardest things to do when somebody has wronged us. We can't find a place in our hearts to forgive the parent who abused us; we can't find a place in our hearts to forgive the combatant enemy who sought to kill us; we can't find the strength to forgive the significant other who cheated on us. Through that lack of forgiveness, we have never been able to let go and accept that those parts of our past are...well, the past. By not letting go through the quality of forgiveness, we have kept resentment, pride, and animosity at the root of the deepest part of who we are.

Above and beyond forgiving others, we often times haven't forgiven ourselves. We haven't forgiven ourselves for not fighting back against the parent whom we watched hit our younger siblings. We haven't forgiven ourselves for coming home from war when others were not given that opportunity. We haven't forgiven ourselves for being so blind that we missed the blatant clues that our spouse was less than honorable in their actions when we weren't looking. We haven't forgiven ourselves for missing the yellow light and running the red, costing a friend or a perfect stranger their lives. We haven't forgiven ourselves for many things that we wish we could find the strength to.

Forgive. Just let go and forgive. It's okay. It's okay to let go of that resentment. It's okay to let go of that hate. It's definitely okay to let go of that guilt—especially that guilt. Forgiving others for what they have done may hurt. It takes true humility and contrition to say, "Hey, I forgive you for what you did to me," but it's worth it. It takes even more humility to say, "I forgive me for what I didn't do, should have done, or did."

With regard to forgiving ourselves, chances are that there is nothing to forgive, but we have harbored the hurt regardless. If there is something to forgive, do it anyway, because the result of not forgiving oneself or others has the same results—it holds us captive and away from spiritual progress.

You see, when we don't forgive, we see our skeletons everywhere we go. We see our abusive fathers in our husbands. We see our cheating ex-wives in every first date. We see an enemy combatant in every person who is of the same nationality that we fought. We see a worthless individual when we look in the mirror. It's not healthy, and it only creates destructive behaviors, relationships, and results.

Imagine looking the person standing before you after he has caused you so much harm that you are sure to die. As you are doing so, you look away from him and toward God and say, "Forgive him, Father, for he knows know not what he does," (Luke 23:34). If Jesus Christ could do that very thing and we look to him as a role model for what being meek and humble is, should we not look daily to find forgiveness for those we harbor ill feelings toward until it is found and given?

When we do in fact find that forgiveness, we are not only forgiving, but liberating. We are liberating our emotions, our past, and, most of all, our future. We will be able to look in the mirror tomorrow and see somebody who can love, who is worthwhile, and who values their very self. We can talk about how the day is going with a stranger we used to only see as the enemy. We can love our spouses for who they are, without resentment for who we think we see. We can sit across from that first date and see a brand new possibility.

Through forgiveness, we allow the future we pave to be free of the skeletons of our past, the ghosts in our closet, and the fears that have driven our daily negative decisions for so long. When we forgive, we move on. When we move on, our possibilities are limited only to our hopes, dreams, and aspirations.

* *

Take advantage of the fact that there is an endless capacity to love. For as long as we have held the negative emotions we have, we should know full well that we can always get madder, angrier, more upset, or sadder. We also know we can dish out more resentment, more adverse responses, and more discontent. There is always room for more.

Imagine if we took all that energy and transformed it into love! Love is one simple emotion that takes the same amount of energy, but yields much more positive results in both ourselves and our relationships. When we look at our fellow man, a stranger, a loved one, or someone we used to find abhorrent, we should search for that same love that we have been given by God and by those who have made us feel good in life. When we give off that aura, the return on investment might surprise us!

When we are able to smile more, when we look for the good things in life that happen rather than dwell on the negative, and when we treat all people we come in contact with kindness, we naturally feel better about ourselves. What's more, we will find that the same type of positivity we exude will surround us. We are able to find other people who can interact positively with us. We become able to create relationships that are happier and healthier, and we find better people within us.

I remember when I was first taught this concept. It was a mix of the art of mindfulness (which is a concept in and of itself), kindness, and acting myself into thinking. I thought, *Yeah, okay. This is kind of cheesy*. However, when I let my "man guard" down, when I put away all prejudgments I had about the concept, I found an inner peace that I had never experienced.

I strongly encourage you to do that same thing. Be kind to yourself and love yourself first and foremost. Be kind and mild-mannered to those you come in contact with, family, friends, and strangers. Perform random acts of kindness daily. Say hi to a perfect stranger daily. If they don't say hi back, that's okay. Call family and friends regularly just to say hi and ask how they are doing. Let them do the talking, but encourage positive topics. Continually ask those you have relationships with, "Is there anything I can do for you?" If they say no, you tried; if they say yes, follow through. The list of examples could go on, but the concept is simple: Exude good, do good, be good.

Lastly, the greatest act of love for those in need is going to be offered when we find a place in our hearts that allows us to feel confident in what we are doing. When we find that place in life, when we see the good in ourselves, we feel what happiness and serenity truly means. We can forgive readily, and we feel a true change in our hearts. It's time to help those who are where we were.

There is no greater therapy I have found than to be there for people who are where I have been. When a veteran with PTSD who struggles with anger management and paranoia wants to talk about it with somebody who understands, I've been there. When he tells me his story, I relate mine and show him the path I found that led me away from the negativity. When a friend is having problems with a relationship, he tells me his story; I can relate mine to his and tell him what I think and the things he should consider while never offering him what I think is the ultimate solution—that is his to find. Going to the homes of fellow church families and sharing gospel messages and how they have personally impacted me is also very fulfilling.

When I do these things, I feel better and better each time. When we all get to that place where we can help those who are in various stages through which we have already passed, we can all feel that same gratification—it's the gratification of offering sincere selflessness, and it should be welcome, as it is truly loving our fellow man through action.

* *

While we have discussed the ten principles I have found most helpful in my walk toward a better Nick, they are not all-inclusive. Books could be written on each topic, and books could be written on hundreds more.

Whether you use all these principles or just some of them, I hope this book has been helpful in starting a new way of life for you. What's most important is that we all find a path toward our own happiness not felt recently, or maybe ever. In short, I hope these principles are useful and help us open the door to those many, many other principles that can help us create better people within ourselves.

As we go through life, we will have struggles. We will have times in which the tears in our eyes come from the depths of our hearts. We will not be perfect in our progress toward betterment. However, keep in mind that progress is a mindset, not a concrete set of rules placed on a document for us to check off. Struggles can be seen as obstacles, not barriers, and the pains we feel should only enhance the happiness we experience in moments of joy.

It took me time in jail, extreme public humiliation, and loss of so much in order to find my path, but I found it. For me, it's in working hard, church participation, working to be a good husband, father, and Christian, and helping others. Quite frankly, for me, it's in the simple things life offers.

Whatever happiness is for you, find it, chase it, attain it, and embrace it. It's there. The only thing in the way is you.

CPSIA information can be obtained at www.ICGtesting.com
Printed in the USA
LVOW11s1133291115

463907LV00005BB/7/P

9 781457 540769